YESTERDAY'S WITNESS

YESTERDAY'S WITNESS

A selection from the BBC series

James Cameron

British Broadcasting Corporation

Published by the
British Broadcasting Corporation
35 Marylebone High Street
London W1M 4AA

ISBN 0 563 17185 5

First published 1979

Printed in England by
Tonbridge Printers Limited

Contents

Introduction

There is this curious period of experience that lies between Now and History, that is not yet wholly remote enough to forget nor so close that it is easy to remember; anthologists' shorthand for this is the Day Before Yesterday.

Taking a more Olympian view of time, we call it simply Yesterday, since by our definition it must lie within living recollection, albeit sometimes, to be sure, only just. There is a very nice distinction between Lloyd George Knew My Father and I Marched From Jarrow – not, indeed, that one precludes the other. Lloyd George would seem to have known everybody's father, and may well have had the role himself often enough. But those who actively remember the Cornish disaster at the Levant tin-mine are few, and growing fewer, as are the men who flew the planes in the First World War. That was why their testimony had to go on the record while it could.

There was never anything in the past to encapsulate the passing of time so exactly, so incontrovertibly and so surely as the film camera and the magnetic tape. What Mr Gladstone said in 1868 we shall never exactly know, but what Mr Churchill said in the 1940s we shall know only too well, and if we don't the archives will remind us.

I am myself a passing indifferent student of true history, but I have had an obsessive preoccupation with that part of it that passed before my own eyes in my own time, and by inference all that is contained in our own century – which basically is the scope and undertaking of our book. We are dealing with my time and your time, or at least that of our fathers, our uncles, even our grandfathers, and everything has a meaning perceptible today.

Old times moved at a leisurely and dignified measure; it was a long time between happenings. The pace of history quickens; the punctuation-marks of our progress, big and little, follow more swiftly on each other's heels; whether we like it or not we live in an age of competing headlines and conflicting considerations: a restless business.

This book has of course nothing to do with all that. That is to say, sometimes it has and sometimes it hasn't. Yesterday's Witnesses were occasionally the witnesses of meaningful and momentous events, happenings that wrote themselves in the larger legends of the country; frequently their involvement was with something that only now seems dramatic, seminal, or even merely quaint, but which without their personal witness might easily have slipped through the net of history and become no more than folk-memory.

More than seventy 'Yesterday's Witnesses' have been made and shown by the BBC: a significant contribution to the record of our times. All were produced by Stephen Peet, a diligent and dedicated film-maker and in some ways an exasperating perfectionist, which I am allowed to say because he is my good friend. He has been the element of continuity throughout this strange charivaria of memories that he has evoked and brought to life. The programmes were directed and written by a variety of people; I had the privilege of working on one or two of them myself.

Their scope has been broad indeed, ranging from great developments like the pioneering of flight and the creation of radio to intensely local group-memories like the Burston School Strike. Some of the people involved have been witnesses to nothing particular except their own lives, like Berta Ruck and Frances Jones, who just define an age eight decades away, and a manner of living that they were among the last to remember, and who could articulate it over the vanished years.

The 'Yesterday's Witness' team is not a sociological or research unit, motivational or otherwise; there are no blueprints, and no preconditions, other than the Yesterday's Witnesses should themselves have been part of the substance of their testimony. There is no second-hand stuff here. What granddad said is not evidence. The localities of these encounters were as varied as the narratives, wherever possible on the relevant spot. Recording studios inspire no memories; rather do they paralyse them. The film people pursued the Yesterday's Witnesses to their homes as relentlessly as Jehovah's Witnesses pursue us to ours. Often enough the people could say: 'It happened just over there, see, at the end of the street.' That was a great help to all sides.

However, I am obliged to intrude an odd consideration here.

I was told that someone once did good business outside the cinemas showing 'Jesus Christ Superstar' by selling Bibles as 'The Book of the Film'. This is not quite the same thing, although the motivation is not dissimilar.

The process of turning a written story into a coherent film is pretty complex, involving many different crafts and skills and rows and disputes and sulks and compromises. The reverse process of turning an essentially visual product back into words is even more awkward, or so it seems to me, since one is at once stripped of a dimension. The working scripts themselves would be silly, burdened as they are with all the technical humbug demanded by film-makers, even those as considerate and reasonable as my learned leader S. Peet.

To attempt to re-create the experience as a literary exercise would be pretentious and even misleading; the whole point of 'Yesterday's Witness' is that the witness is spontaneous and idiosyncratic and often quite dotty.

I have tried to steer a middle course, as far as possible, defining the theme, setting the scene of the episodes, and letting the characters rip, with their own words in their own fashion, with perhaps an occasional nudge along the way.

After all, these are their stories.

No to the Army

Conscientious Objectors at a special camp in 1916

The First World War began in the summer of 1914, and within 18 months had cut a swathe through a generation of the youth of Europe.

At the start every soldier in the British Army was a professional, a volunteer. By 1916 tens of thousands of them were dead. The lunacies of the great Commanders had squandered them, and killed them, and used them up. So more, less willing, had to be found.

The answer was Conscription. By May 1916 all able-bodied men between 18 and 41 were obliged, by law, to join the Army.

For many it was a dire crisis of conscience. Many, indeed 16,000 or so – refused to obey the law. They were called Conscientious Objectors – sometimes, derisively, Conchies. It was a conscience they had to prove, to a Tribunal, and hard it was to do. Some were socialists, who opposed this particular war. Some were Quakers, who denied the principle of war itself. Some were well-to-do, some were poor; the common ground was that each was an individual opposing the State because, as he felt, he had no choice.

Because of their belief 73 C.O.s died, in jail or soon thereafter; 31 went mad. Some survived.

JACK FOISTER Court martialled simply for refusing to fall in behind a corporal. That was the technical offence and we then faced the question – well, are you prepared to carry this opposition to war to the point of being shot for your conviction?

HARRY STANTON When my turn came, the man who got the papers was standing near to me, and I could see on the top of the paper in very big capital letters: 'DEATH' in red ink, and I thought: 'Oh well, I'm being treated differently. . . .'

HAROLD BING I would say that a conscientious objector is a man who as a result of inner conviction which may be, of course, religious, moral or philosophical, feels that it is impossible for him to kill his fellow men deliberately, and therefore take part in war or the preparation for war in any kind of military service. It involves a strong sense of moral obligation, that this thing is wrong for me, though it may be right for other people.

ALFRED CORUM Well, I felt it was a battle of imperialism for the division of the markets of the world and I felt it had nothing to do with the working class, and therefore wouldn't take part in it.

FRANK MERRICK I felt very strongly that I would much rather be shot than shoot anyone else.

HARRY STANTON I was a Quaker and used to thinking in terms of, that war was wrong thing for men to engage in. I felt that the mass of people felt that war was right, but my conviction was different and that I had to testify as best I could.

FENNER BROCKWAY It wasn't only the Quakers who took what was the absolutist position, it was very many of us who were not only not Quakers, but whose objection was mostly on political grounds and the No Conscription Fellowship was actually formed before the military service acts and began by opposing conscription.

Fenner Brockway (later Lord Brockway) was instrumental in forming the No-Conscription Fellowship which was to be the focal point of the Conscientious Objectors' movement until the end of the war. It advised men on behaviour before the Tribunals set up under the Military Service Act of 1916.

ALLEN SKINNER It was not only a humiliation, it was quite an ordeal going before the first tribunal, and this I think was quite typical. I had unfortunately used the word 'fundamental' in the second line of my statement, and the chairman of the tribunal started reading it, and he boggled at the word fundamental, and couldn't get it out, and with a grunt of dissatisfaction pushed the thing on one side so that my statement was never read.

HAROLD BING There was the case of a man who, for a bet, said he could go before a tribunal and prove that he was a conscientious objector, though in fact he wasn't. And he went before a tribunal and putting up a very slick case managed to convince the tribunal that he was an objector and was granted exemption. He then thanked the Chairman of the tribunal, and said that he'd done it merely for a bet, and he was now going to join the Army. This, of course, proves the impossibility for a tribunal to judge the sincerity of a conscientious objection.

HARRY STANTON They were to a certain extent sympathetic . . . the military representative wasn't sympathetic, but they offered me exemption if I would take up work under a public body. I said well, what would be the purpose of that, would it be to release somebody else to go into the army? They hadn't got an answer to that. I said well, it's quite clear that's the purpose, and I can't accept it.

Many objectors refused non-combatant service for that reason. More than 6000 were therefore duly arrested as deserters.

The No-Conscription Fellowship made sure its members knew what to expect; they were well briefed. They knew that they would be ordered to put on uniform, and that it was imperative to refuse.

MARK HAYLER In my case they took my clothes away, the civilian clothes, and left me with the uniform hoping I'd put it on. Well, it was one of the things one didn't do, you see. I remember on one occasion my father coming to see me and all I had on was an overcoat.

F. J. MURFIN We'd a man to strip us and dress us, and when it came to the socks the one who was dressing me said 'You put your socks on mate, your feet smell'.

HARRY STANTON I just held myself limp and they had to carry me about and lift me up and put my trousers on. It was quite amusing in its way, though I was sorry for the NCOs who had to do it, because they'd been showing off a bit before, swearing what they'd do to us.

MARK HAYLER And other times we wore the uniforms inside out, turned the coats inside out, since we had to wear something. In those kinds of ways you had to let the military know that you were not co-operating with them.

HOWARD MARTEN The whole thing was remarkably strange, you didn't know what the future held. And after being what they called forcibly dressed, it was more or less—'Well, you've been ordered to dress us; we'll make the thing as easy as we can for you.' I always personally wanted to avoid anything in the way of making things difficult for those who had to handle you. And in the same way to officers; 'Well I've got to disobey your orders, I don't intend you personally any discourtesy'.

FENNER BROCKWAY About 3000 soldiers all lined up to hear my sentence, I think as a warning to them. As my sentence of, I think, two years hard labour was read out, I stood forward and in a voice which was accustomed to speak in the open air, I said 'I shall be very proud to do it, sir'. The soldiers all shivered, and while I was kicked all the way back to the guardroom by my sergeant, from that moment there was some admiration, and some appreciation. Then as the war went on, there was much more sympathy from the soldiers.

In 1916 the Army decided to make a serious example of some men, and began quietly to move them up to the lines, where they would be very vulnerable. Out of England meant technical active service, where the death penalty applied.

HOWARD MARTEN All the time, we were being threatened by various officials and officers; 'If you persist in this attitude, well, you're going to be shot'. 'And You'll be taken where your friends won't be able to do anything for you'. That was a very favourite remark. We were much more concerned about the attitude we must take. The consequences didn't enter into it. Well, then we found ourselves at the Harwich redoubt, sentenced to 28 days detention.

ALFRED EVANS Harwich redoubt is a fortress sunk inside the hill, you can't tell anything about it from the outside, except from the gateways from the road. These cells were absolutely pitch dark and running with water. The rats ran over us and the water streamed down the place, absolutely pitch black, there wasn't a light to be seen anywhere.

Thirty-four Conscientious Objectors were sent to France. When they arrived by troopship in Le Havre, F. J. Murfin had to give his name.

F. J. MURFIN He started calling me Private Murfin, and I said 'I'm not a private'. He says 'You are a private' and we went on like that for a bit, and I said 'You can think I am if you like, but I'm not a private, I'm a prisoner.' Then he pointed out to his one arm missing, and he said 'I lost that defending you'. I says 'You didn't. You lost that trying to destroy somebody else', which made him very cross.

JACK FOISTER I don't know whether I'm ridiculous, but when I went out to France I'd no idea of military life of any sort, and I did imagine that an officer would order me to do something and I would just decline to do it, and he would shoot me. I didn't think there were such things as trials for people who were mutinous, as they styled it.

HARRY STANTON We were tied to posts with a wooden frame going across, and we were tied to it with our arms like this. It wasn't very comfortable, and the next day a young Canadian came up to me and started asking me questions about my family, and who there was at home, my mother and my sister and so on. Of course there I was stuck up against this post, and he saw I was beginning to weep a little at the thought of my people at home, and so he came up and got my handkerchief out of somewhere or other, and wiped my eyes, which I thought was very striking for this young fellow to do. Well, that evening we were crucified again, but this time to barbed wire. Of course, tying you to barbed wire, you get tied very much more tightly than to a big wooden joist, and we were tied so tightly my face was practically right up against the barbed wire, I couldn't turn my head without scratching it on the barbed wire.

MILES MALLESON To feel angry about it is awfully difficult, because God knows the Conscientious Objectors, and the men who went into the trenches all suffered bloody hell, and they all showed an awful lot of bravery. And one doesn't want to set one against the other.

HOWARD MARTEN And I think it would be doing the pacifist cause an ill service to exaggerate any physical discomfort that we were subjected to.

Finally there came the courts martial. The Objectors were charged with wilful disobedience to lawful orders.

ALFRED EVANS Just before the court martial, an officer, a captain in the Notts and Derbys, came to see me, and he said 'I've just come out of the Company office, Evans', he said, 'I've been looking through your papers, they're marked death in red at the top'. He said 'Do you intend to go on with this?' I said 'Yes. You see, sir, while we're talking, there are men dying in agony for the things they believe in, I wouldn't be less than them'. To my astonishment, he stood back a couple of paces and saluted me, and then came forward and shook hands.

JACK FOISTER It went on for about a fortnight, I suppose, the first court martial, the second court martial about a week later, and then a week after that I should think the four of us were taken up to Henriville camp where there was a tremendous parade of all the non-combatant corps, I think it was, the work part of the army, not the fighting part, lined round this camp, thousands of them, we were in the centre, just the four of us.

HOWARD MARTEN Then I was called out to the front and after the charge had been read out 'The sentence of the Court was that you are to suffer death by being shot'. Then there was a pause. 'But afterwards commuted to penal servitude for ten years.'

JACK FOISTER Jonathan Ring turned to me – he was a Socialist and I was a Socialist – as soon as Howard Marten's sentence was read out, he said 'He's a Friend. If they'll do that to Friends, they'll shoot us'.

HOWARD MARTEN I think one lost a sense . . . I began to lose a sense of personality. You felt you were part of something outside yourself.

One after another these Objectors heard their death sentences commuted. They seem to have escaped the firing squad because their own organisation in London, the N-C.F., had moved fast. It confronted Asquith with the fact that the Army had shipped these men to France. Asquith claimed to know nothing of this, and that in any case the Army had no authority to shoot them. Professor Gilbert Murray went to see Lord Derby, the Minister of Recruiting, who said the Army had every right to shoot anyone disobeying orders. He added: 'And serve them right.'

Asquith was appalled, and sent an order forbidding the executions.

The men were classed as convicts, and sent home to civil prisons. Soon there were several thousand prisoners of conscience in British jails. That had never happened before.

F. J. MURFIN We spoke so that you didn't move your lips, so this man said 'What's your name?' I said 'Fred, what's yours?' 'Joe'. 'How long have you got?' 'Ten years. How long have you got?' 'Ten years.' 'What're you in for?' Says 'Conscientious Objector'. 'What the bloody hell's that?' So I tried to explain. All this took a long while of course. I says 'What are you in for, Joe?' 'Murder'. I said 'That's funny, isn't it'. 'What's funny?' I says 'Well, you got ten years for killing somebody – and I expect you were drunk – and I've got ten years because I won't kill anybody.'

Six thousand Conscientious Objectors in jail constituted a highly-organised and articulate body – organised despite the ban on organisation; articulate in spite of the rule of silence, the prohibition of prison conversation. They devised their own stratagems.

ALLEN SKINNER I came into chapel beside Arthur Haycock, who was subsequently M.P. for Salford. I stood beside him and when it came to the hymn, what I heard coming from Haycock's lips was 'Have you heard that George Benson came in yesterday'. That was the chap who's now Sir George Benson, he was another Manchester man too.

FENNER BROCKWAY We had other means of communication. We had a hot pipe system going from cell to cell, and even going to the floors above. We had a complete telephone situation. We all learned the morse code in reverse, and by tapping on the pipe and giving the number of the cell we wanted, it was exactly like a telephonic communication. We could even be put on to the floor above. But all the time there was the danger of being discovered, of bread and water, and one always had a certain amount of fear of this. And I came to the conclusion that we ought to resist the silence rule openly. And for ten wonderful days at Liverpool prison we ran our hall, there would be about 60 conscientious objectors there. We made our own rules. We talked openly, and when we went on exercise, instead of marching round in a circle five feet behind each other, we went arm in arm and talked. We were shut in our cells, we made our own rules when there would be silence for reading. Every night we had concerts and lectures by someone speaking through an open window, and his voice could be heard the whole length. This had a serious effect upon other prisoners. And after ten days, the five leaders of what was described as mutiny, were deported to other prisons.

Many of the prisons had their own underground newspapers. One of them, the Winchester Whisperer, was edited by Alfred Corum.

ALFRED CORUM I started that as a prison paper, of course quite surreptitiously, and it ran for some 12 or 13 issues. One every month or so. It was made up on toilet paper. I had a small piece of copying pencil which I wrote out the material with, and then I damped it. Then I handed it to somebody who bound it, and then it was circulated by hand. There was some very good material in it, because there were some very good people in prison.

The authorities got wind of it and made two or three thorough searches of the prison but they never discovered it. The Chaplain who came round one evening . . . he came round on press night, and I had the whole issue hung up behind my cell door on a line to dry, and he opened the door and came in. Are you all right? Yes. What are you reading? Oh, the Bible. So he went out. He little knew how near he was to discovering the Winchester Whisperer.

The prison authorities unwittingly provided the paper for the publications, but still the pencil leads had to be smuggled in.

FENNER BROCKWAY We found one way by which, even when you were stripped, you could get leads into prison by putting them under the arch of the foot, and I stepped into the bath, and to my horror the water started to go purple. I'd got purple leads. When the warder came up and saw the water purple, he told off a prisoner who, fortunately, was a conscientious objector, for having put disinfectant in the water, said I was not a hospital case, and so I got away with it.

AYLMER ROSE In the prison where I was I found that about half the warders were members of the Independent Labour Party, and this was especially true of the workmaster who looked after the prison painting and repairs and decorating – all that sort of thing. And men who worked in his squad saw the Labour Party papers every week.

HAROLD BING I can instance the case for example of one warder who became almost converted to the pacifist point of view, and with whom I had quite a friendly relationship. In fact, he used to open my cell door early in the morning and slip in his daughter's homework for me to check.

MARK HAYLER That was at Wandsworth. My mother brought me a rose from the garden, but they took it from me. I don't know whether they thought I'd cut my throat with it or what.

HAROLD BING I suppose that after a time one began to suffer a sort of mental and nervous hibernation, that is to say one's senses became dulled, one accepted the routine, one ceased to think or react very much. One lost one's consciousness of unity with the world outside, and adapted oneself to the prison environment, and made the best of it.

JACK FOISTER I was never got down by tedium. I could always find something to do. I would do daft things like counting up all the letters in the Bible and making a list to show their frequencies.

FENNER BROCKWAY I invented a little football game with buttons.

ALFRED CORUM I wrote on toilet paper, and in the back pages of a book, a sonata for piano. It is dated as you see Winchester 1917-Plymouth 1920. It's never had any success because I've never got anybody to study it. There were other works as well I managed to get out on scraps of toilet paper, string quartets and so on.

After a while the Home Office granted the concession – largely to conciliate the uneasy public – that these men, if they satisfied a tribunal, could go outside and do useful work, or so-called useful work.

HARRY STANTON We were taken from the prison and put in all sorts of odd clothing and sent up to Scotland to a place near Aberdeen called Dyce, which was a worked out quarry. There were great lumps of granite about which needed to be crushed in the granite crushers, suitable for road making.

MARK HAYLER The shovels and the spades and the picks all had lead down the shafts, so that they should be heavy, you see; part of the hard labour, I suppose. We did a lot of stone breaking while we were there. We went out on to the moors on agricultural work and dug in fields. It took a hundred or so of us to dig a huge field which could have been ploughed in a few hours. But there again it was the kind of work they put us to – wasteful employment.

HARRY STANTON Many of us were very uneasy about the whole business, and after a while we said we weren't going to continue with this, so we wrote to the Home Office and said we weren't satisfied to continue under this, would they arrange for us to go back to prison.

In fact the stonebreakers in Aberdeenshire learned later that they had been hoodwinked into building a military road.

The State began to release the objectors under an amnesty in the spring of 1919. At once came the howls from the Press that these men were snatching jobs from the nation's heroes. This was of course far from the case; a record as a Conscientious Objector was a serious handicap in finding work.

So what did these men achieve?

AYLMER ROSE Looking at it now, I would say that we demonstrated that it is impossible to break the spirit of men who are really convinced; that's the first thing. The second thing is that we had written conscientious objector, conscientious objection, permanently into the law of England.

HAROLD BING If one regards the State as a merely human institution, liable to all sorts of failures and errors, then one adopts a critical attitude and places the authority of conscience before that of the State. This point of view has been strengthened internationally by the judgments of the Nuremberg Tribunal which, of course, laid it down that in the case of war crimes, a man cannot plead obedience to the State or the Law, or his superior officers, as a defence against any crimes which he may commit. Each person is morally responsible for his own acts, and this in fact is an endorsement of the position of the conscientious objector, though it was not intended as such by the Judges at Nuremberg.

FENNER BROCKWAY When the Military Training Act was endorsed before the last world war, the Government made it clear that they didn't want to repeat the persecution during the First World War. And undoubtedly in the Second World War conscientious objectors were treated more generously. It not only had its effect on the liberty for conscience in this country, but I think all over the world.

The Burning of the Bombing School

D. J. Williams, photographed in 1970

Towards the end of his life, which came about not long ago, D. J. Williams, schoolmaster and Welshman, claimed he had been privileged to have been a member of three Universities: the Welsh University of Aberystwyth, then Jesus College, Oxford, and finally and most importantly Wormwood Scrubs in the capital of the British Empire.

D. J. Williams was imprisoned for arson. This was back in 1936, when he and two friends, Saunders Lewis and Lewis Valentine, set fire to £2000 worth of Government property, set – immorally, as they argued – on the soil of Wales.

D. J. WILLIAMS In the spring of 1932 there was an International Disarmament Conference under the auspices of the League of Nations held in Geneva. And at that conference it was the almost unanimous opinion of all the nations there that aerial bombardment of innocent citizens in towns and cities was too horrible a thing to be allowed to go on. Strangely, perhaps, the strongest dissenter to this idea of banning aerial bombardment was Great Britain itself. The result was that after about a year the conference broke up without anything worth while being done at all.

Meanwhile, however, the Government needed a site on which to train bomber crews.

The first choice was Abbotsbury, in Dorset. There were immediate protests on behalf of the famous Abbotsbury swans. The Government withdrew, and announced that their bombing school would be on Holy Island, in Northumberland. Again there were protests: Holy Island was a bird sanctuary, home of a rare breed of duck.

The Government chose a third site – on Lleyn Peninsular in North Wales. And here there were no swans and no ducks – only the human beings of Wales.

D. J. WILLIAMS A law-abiding, faithful nation, always loyal to the Empire in its day of need – surely this nation would oblige, and take the site of an aerodrome or bombing school within their territory? In 1935, when this project was finally decided upon, public opinion straight away became forcible against the very idea. A quiet and unspoilt area like Lleyn where the Welsh language was at its purist – this spot was picked upon for a site of an aerodrome! The whole nation stood on its feet in protest against it.

The protests grew over the year. Meetings were held, posters paraded through the streets. The Secretary of the Welsh Nationalists prayed the Prime Minister to receive a deputation, Mr Stanley Baldwin refused.

D. J. WILLIAMS The swannery in Abbotsbury and the duckery in Northumberland had been sufficiently powerful means of desisting the English Government from going on; well, there was nothing for us to do but to take direct action. Three of us were selected to do the job, of whatever nature. Saunders Lewis, Senior Lecturer in Welsh at the time, Reverend L. E. Valentine, one of the most popular preachers and best known public figure in Wales. And I was the third.

So we three met on Monday night, 7 September 1936 and decided to do what we thought was our duty. Namely, to set the aerodrome site on fire. It was not an act of vandalism, but a direct protest in the name of the whole

Welsh Nation, in order that we could plead our case in a public court of law.

So the decision was taken to set fire to the bombing school under construction, to expose their protest to public debate.

There were four other colleagues, whose orders were that they should not be identified or captured. J. E. Jones was one of them, on that night of 7 September 1936.

D. J. WILLIAMS My particular spot of setting on fire was a shed. It was a windy night. I had only one box and I used every match that I had, and I failed to get the fire going. So I had to go to my friend Valentine to borrow some more matches, but they failed. Anyhow it was too windy for that to take place.

However, other matches worked. The three amateur arsonists walked over the hill to the police-station at Pwllheli, and asked to be arrested for starting a fire the police did not even know was burning.

D. J. WILLIAMS The police were very decent, fair play to them. We told them what we had done and they wouldn't believe it. And we were trying to remember a well known sonnet written by a friend of ours, one of the finest poets in Wales, his name was Williams Parry, and we three couldn't remember the sonnet very completely. One of the constables on duty who was better informed than we were, he helped us out, and we between the four of us we got the sonnet completely recited.

Many people in Wales were behind this protest action, but many were not. In Pwllheli local feeling was very much against it. For them the bombing school meant work – badly-needed jobs with a firm of Scottish contractors. One of the Scotsmen continued to live in the area for years.

SCOTSMAN We thought it was an accidental fire until we found petrol cans and sprays lying about. They'd gave themselves up and when they came out of court they were almost mobbed by the population of this town. Because the population thought it was a disgraceful thing to do (voice: which is right!) for it was the first time the local men and around the area had a decent job and decent pay to go to.

However that may have been, by the time the case reached the Assize Court at Caernarvon the town was crammed with supporters.

CATRIN DANIEL The scene at the court was quite extraordinary. The judge, whether we imagined it or not, he looked a little apprehensive, because I think the streets of Caernarvon were so crowded and the noise outside was so menacing that the judge grew more nervous as the trial wore on. There was deathly silence in the court as the three men made their defence, and when applause broke out, the judge got extremely nasty and rebuked Saunders Lewis several times for arousing enthusiasm in the court.

J. E. JONES I was in court, of course. I had copies of their speeches. In fact, they had been printed and were sold after the court hours that evening by their thousands. Time and time again Judge Lewis, who was very antagonistic, he would stop Saunders Lewis and Lewis Valentine and say 'It isn't relevant' and they would reply 'I'm sorry, my Lord, I thought it was relevant, I will go on to the next point'. But they didn't go on to the next point, they went on with the next word, every time, and so the jury heard the entire speeches. No, not the entire speeches. Lewis Valentine was nearing the end of his speech, when once again the judge interfered. And Lewis Valentine said: 'My Lord you are interfering so often that I cannot go on, I will sit down'. I had a copy of the speech, he had left out *two words* only at the end of his speech.

The jury were out for 90 minutes, and then the Judge asked the foreman: 'Are you agreed on a verdict?' And the foreman replied: 'Yes, my lord, we have failed to agree.'

There was nothing for it but to order a retrial, in the Old Bailey.

CATRIN DANIEL This was on the grounds that local feeling at Caernarvon had prejudiced the jury favourably towards the prisoners. Everybody knew we hadn't a hope of success at the Old Bailey.

D. J. WILLIAMS Saunders Lewis and Valentine refused to give their evidence in any language but their own, in Welsh. And that wasn't allowed, so they didn't say a word at all. But as it happened, no one of the prosecutors had heard me speak any English at all, with the result that I was allowed to speak in Welsh. I refused to defend myself, only made a protest against my being removed from amongst my fellow countrymen. But the funny part about it was that I had been English Master in the Fishguard Grammar School for fifteen years, and nobody knew apparently that I knew any English.

CATRIN DANIEL The Old Bailey was so different, you see. At Caernarvon all of us had felt that we were involved in an historical situation – this Welsh trial and the very English judge; you felt that you really were alive to all the forces that were pitted one against the other. But at the Old Bailey suddenly these men simply appeared as rather eccentric malefactors. And that was the end of it, it was completely flat and colourless.

Not everyone in Court was a Nationalist by any means. Miss Berta

Ruck, the romantic novelist, thought the accused were just self-conscious martyrs.

BERTA RUCK They all pretended that they couldn't speak a word of English. One of them was then a school teacher from Fishguard who spoke English probably better than any of us. In the most courtly and courteous manner the Judge said: 'Mr Interpreter, will you tell the accused that I am not here to determine whether or not they are unhappy under English rule, I am here merely to hear whether they have been destroying property.' And then he passed sentence, which was nine months each. Their wives were told that they might go and speak to them before they were led down to the cells. All the wives refused with indignation. 'We will not accept any favour from this government!' So they went out into the street outside the Old Bailey and immediately burst into song. The police were very tactful. They said if you go round that back street there they will be able to hear you in prison; they can't hear you from here, there's too much traffic. So they went round, and you presently heard (sings) 'Hen Wlad fy Nhadau' and all that sort of thing. And, you know, I've been to a good many theatres in my time, but I never enjoyed anything so much as I enjoyed this pantomime.

But there for the schoolmaster, the lecturer, and the minister, the pantomime ended, in prison.

D. J. WILLIAMS On the whole we found the Warders very human. Worse thing there perhaps was the food. Both Valentine and I lost 22 lbs in weight during the nine months that we were there.

The governor of the gaol, he was very decent all along and he called us to him on the night of our departure and thanked the three of us for our good influence upon the community in which we had found ourselves.

There was a vast welcome-home meeting for the three men in the Great Pavilion at Caernarvon, the biggest hall to be found in Wales. It held 12,000 people, and it was packed.

CATRIN DANIEL I certainly remember the singing of 'The Men of Harlech', I never heard anything sung like this at all. The enthusiasm and the sense of conviction was something which could only be compared to a revival meeting, you know, in the great days of religion. Of course one is never sure how deep these things go. There certainly were few fruits of it to be seen afterwards in solid achievement. But, you see, we were on the eve of World War II.

Meanwhile, work went on at the bombing school, and a year later it opened.

And then it was discovered – as might have been divined before – that the thick sea mists of West Wales made the Lleyn Peninsular totally unsuitable for bombing training. Four years later it just closed.

The Great Blizzard of 1891

Kingsbridge, Devon, the day after the blizzard of 1891

One quiet spring morning in 1891, in the West Country of England, it suddenly began to snow.

Very soon it was clear that there had never been recorded snow like this before, nor has been since.

A contemporary account of the great blizzard begins: 'On the morning of 9th March 1891, when the inhabitants of the three westernmost counties of England were preparing for the routine duties of daily life, nothing indicated that the gravest atmospheric disturbance of the century would come to spread terror and destruction.'

This was no ordinary storm; it was a freak phenomenon, an Arctic blizzard of hurricane force that endured on and off for more than three days – flattening forests, burying thousands of sheep and cattle, lashing the sea into extraordinary fury. Around Devon and Cornwall alone more than 40 ships and boats were wrecked; more than a hundred seamen lost their lives. Twenty-three trains were derailed or snowed up for days; the roads became impassable for weeks.

Tom Trebilcock was ten at the time. He went to the village school at Devoran in South Cornwall. That March day began so warm they could sit taking their dinners outside.

TOM TREBILCOCK We hadn't been in very long, probably an hour, when the light begin to fade, and then it went dimmer and dimmer and we could scarcely see. The headmaster went out and discovered it was snowing thick, so he dismissed school and ordered us to hurry home as fast as possible. The snow was blinding. And after we'd had our tea, father went out and brought in two shovels and a broom. I couldn't quite understand why.

By evening the blizzard was raging all over the West Country. In the Devon village of Stokenham at the end of his day's work was the 14-year-old odd-job boy Alfred Hayman, hoping for his usual lift home by coach to Chillington.

ALFRED HAYMAN Squire Homesworth's keeper come along and said, 'Hello, boy, what thee doing here this time of nit?' So I said, 'Well, I'm waiting for the coach.' 'Ho,' he said, 'Thee wouldn't see no coach yet,' so he see I'm getting a bit worried. 'All right, boy,' he said, 'I'll take thee home.' And we started off. The snow, then, well it got half way up the telegraph posts and when we got up there to Kerry's Cross I could hardly get along at all. He was dressed in a posh coat – that was his livery – and buckskin breeches and leggings – so he said, 'Catch hold of me tails, boy'. So I caught hold of his tails and he dragged me up over the drifts to Chillington.

On the morning of 10 March, on the edge of Dartmoor in the parish of Harford, eight-year-old Ethel Williams and her sister awoke in a world strangely dark.

ETHEL WILLIAMS My father called us to be quiet. Then father got out. He felt uneasy. He went to the window. He couldn't see anything, and he realised it was snow outside. He went downstairs and got mother's long-handled sweeping brush to try and find how deep it was. It was above the eaves of the house. So he kept on until he made a hole big enough to let a little light down. And then he crept out and went to feed the cattle out to the yard.

Up there on the moor hundreds of animals were already dead, or struggling to survive. Sheep panic and run before the wind. Hundreds were buried deep in the snow.

TOM TREBILCOCK And the way the farmers located them was little holes where their breath came up on the surface, their breath turned it yellow, and when they dug down the sheep were in a heap. The top ones were alive but the others had suffocated. On the Bodmin Moors they went miles away in front of the blizzard. The moorland farms went after them, but it was useless because the snow was coming down so thick and fast it covered up all the landmarks and several of these moorland farmers never found their way back. They perished the same as the sheep.

One of the paradoxical problems, in these country cottages almost buried in snow, was getting water.

ETHEL WILLIAMS I remember mother opening the back door and it was all white – you couldn't see anything but snow. And she put a boiler on the floor and gave us tablespoons, and we had to spoon the snow out. We made little holes in the snow and spooned it out into the boiler and she boiled it to get water. I don't remember what it tasted like in the tea or anything – I can't remember that. I suppose she had a certain amount of food in the house – she must of – so I don't remember being hungry. It was the third day in the afternoon by the time we were dug out. And I can remember mother giving me an old pair of stockings to pull on over my boots – we wore boots in those days, not shoes – so that I didn't slip on the snow. And father had made like little steps in some places. We had to sort of creep along. My elder sister went first and I went after. It was only the two of us allowed out at that time. We went along by the tops of the high wall, and it was really that wall of the garden belonging to the old manor house. We were very pleased to be able to look in over that, because we'd often wanted to see over the wall into the garden. Well, we walked a little further until we were standing on snow near a gateway, and it was – well it was beautiful; it was marvellous, really, my sister and I looked at it, and we wondered, we thought God must have made it, because nobody else could.

At sea the storm was not beautiful. More than 40 vessels were lost. In two wrecks alone more than 50 men were drowned.

Gravestones in many churchyards record the shipwreck toll of that week. Alfred Hayman, the odd-job boy at Stokenham vicarage, remembers when five dead and unknown trawlermen were washed up.

ALFRED HAYMAN When the old man came with the coffins on Saturday evening he brought them in a big market cart, there were three in the bottom and two on top. So they unloaded these coffins in the stable-yard and they started putting the bodies in the coffins. The old man was putting in one body and one of the men who was there as a bearer put in another. 'Ho,' other said, 'he won't go in'. 'For why?' 'His boots won't go down.' 'Ho dear, j-j-jump on him, j-j-j-jump on him.' So that's what they done, they jumped on 'em getting in the coffin. Poor chap.

This was long before the days of the ordinary motor-car. There was steam power, but the railways were blocked, there was horse-power, and no roads. There was a young schoolteacher, Mrs Lilian Williams, she went by horse and trap across Bodmin Moor to the little town of Camelford. It was six weeks before she was able to return. But somehow she did. At the age of 102 she still remembered that they managed to eat.

LILIAN WILLIAMS We never seemed to be short. I think the country people generally keep a good bit under hand, in case of emergency. Old fashioned, on the hearth, we used to bake in those days. Open fire . . . put down the round iron . . . and clean it you know. Sprinkle flour over it, and then drop down pasties or buns, loaves of bread. Put piles of hot coals on top and around, and then leave it so low. Open it up and they'd be baked lovely. Taste? Better than the tinned stuff we get now. No tinned stuff in those days. I don't remember that we were short of water. We fetched the water at that time. Nothing piped in the houses then. Very different now.

Spring came very late to the West Country that year, and traces of the great blizzard were slow to go away.

ETHEL WILLIAMS My father came down the lane to dinner. And he'd got a lump of ice under his arm. He had brought it from the quarry, way up near the moor, and he'd brought it home to show us children and he said 'I want you children to come and see this lump of ice because I don't expect you'll ever see the like of this again on Midsummer's Day'.

The Burston School Strike

Tom and Annie Higdon

The English farming countryside, placid and unexcessive, sometimes produces small adventures that do not often make history, but that are so unexpected, so peculiar to the unpredictable English country character that they are worth enshrining for their own uniqueness. The Burston School Strike might have become part of the Labour Party mythology of this century, had it not been overwhelmed by the even more clamant drama of the First World War. As it is, it remains a monument to a little but tremendous local loyalty, as memorable in its quiet way as Tolpuddle.

The village of Burston is just north of Diss, in East Anglia, on the main line to Norwich – not that the trains stop there any more, as once they did. Yet there was a time, some sixty years ago, when Burston's village green was a place of pilgrimage for British Labour people proving solidarity with – of all people – the children of the village school.

In this dull and tranquil corner of Norfolk the local schoolchildren took the most drastic action and spontaneous act of love: they came out on strike because their teachers had been sacked. For a while it became a national issue. And the Burston School Strike went on for *more than twenty years.*

A village schoolroom upset? How could it matter?

It all began in the simplest way. The children of Burston loved their schoolmistress and their schoolmaster. These two were deeply-principled, old-fashioned radicals, of the sternly reasonable Tom Paine kind. Obviously the children did not understand how the political resonances would be heard everywhere.

Annie Higdon was the certified teacher, and her husband Tom Higdon was her assistant. They must have been a truly remarkable couple. They had run the Council School at Burston for three years before their troubles began.

Before that, the Higdons had worked at another school under the same Norfolk Education Committee at a village called Wood Dalling – a straggling little place in poor farming land, where life was all right for the landowners, but not for anyone else. There the wife-and-husband team of the Higdons ran their late-Victorian country school. In those days Ted Williams was a very little boy.

TED WILLIAMS I believe I came to the school when I was four and a half. But Mr Higdon, as far as I can remember, he didn't come here not till 1902, and that left me about seven, you see.

Mrs Higdon used to teach at this end of the school and Mr Higdon, he taught at that end of the school.

There must have been about ninety children at the Wood Dalling school then, the older ones all together in this one room, with Annie and Tom Higdon.

SIDNEY PAYNE In the door would come Mr and Mrs Higdon. We had to stand up and salute and say 'Goodmorning Governess. Goodmorning Sir.' Mr Higdon would call the register, and those who were there at the time would get a red mark; if they came after they closed the register they would get a black one.

Mrs Higdon put everything down in her log-book. She was strict, and she was gentle. Farm-workers' children in those days were the most part very, very poor.

TED WILLIAMS I thought Mrs Higdon was a very kind woman. She was really kind and the poor children in the school, she tried her hardest to get them something – a little extra to what they'd had at home.

JESSIE SPRINGALL There were eleven of us. We didn't see the things like you see today though; we lived on potatoes and just ordinary food. They didn't have the wages, because my father only earned twelve shillings a week.

Mrs Higdon's idea was to help the girls with practical things, like cooking – things with meaning in poor farmworkers' homes. Mrs Higdon did not believe all education came from books.

JESSIE SPRINGALL She learnt us how to make all clothes and things – knitting. That was what was very good of her, because we used to go round and the people were glad to buy them you see. They got them cheaper.

And I can remember if you didn't behave yourselves you got to stand on a stool in front of the class with your hands on your head.

But the Higdons were even sterner with the farmers when they found the children being kept illegally from school to work the fields. There was one day Tom Higdon saw from the school window one of his regular truants working on the land. Everyone remembered that day.

TED WILLIAMS His name was Albert Cotterall and on this very field in front of the school here he was, what we call in Norfolk, leading the horse in the drill, the front horse, and Mr Higdon knew well enough he should be at school. He sent a note asking the farmer to send the boy to school, and nothing happened. I think he sent another note. I heard all this, you see, and so nothing happened and then Tom went after him and he gave the farmer a black eye, you see. 'Course they went to court and they had to pay.

Tom was fined 40 shillings and costs. It was only one of many conflicts. What the local society could not understand was that all the Higdons' unorthodoxy was what they thought best for the children. And clearly it was. The Government Inspectors said they were 'energetic and industrious teachers'. The local managers did not agree.

It is hard to remember how such a short time ago these rural communities were ruled by a combination of patronage and privilege that was almost feudal even then. The school managers were appointed from a little circle of the local bourgeoisie, the petty squirearchy and the parsonage. It wasn't an establishment that would take kindly to the uncompromising consciences of the Higdons, who interpreted 'education' literally, as not to Cram In but to Lead Forth – which in those days necessarily meant socialism. Clearly Mr and Mrs Higson were on a collision course.

MRS RANSOME She would want to have a good fire winter-time because some of us would be practically wet through by the time we got there and there used to be a huge round guard right round the fire and that used to be full of clothes drying off. She used to stir the managers up. And, of course, they used to get so annoyed with her because she would want more coal . . . One thing led to another and then there was, with her husband, a bit of political party attached to it as well because he was always a man, you know, who stuck up for the agricultural workers. The managers were nearly all farmers, that didn't suit them.

The fact is that Tom Higdon was a very political man. He had been working for the new local farm workers' union. In general he got everybody's backs up, and the upshot was that the Norfolk Education Committee told the troublesome Higdons to go. The odd thing is that they passed them on to another school – the one they turned into folk-lore.

On the last day of January 1911 the Higdons took over the Council School of Burston, with 70 or 80 farmworkers' children.

VIOLET POTTER We thought they were the best teachers we'd ever had, you know. They were so, so kind and so talkative to us. Not like the teachers we'd had before. Mrs Higdon was one of those – one of the best. Wonderful things she did for the children. If they came to school with poor boots and they took water, she'd buy them a new pair, all out of her own pocket. She taught us typewriting. She had an old-fashioned typewriter, probably you wouldn't recognise it today, an old Oliver. And she brought that to school, that was her own. Taught some of us bigger children to use that.

We'd meet up the schoolhouse, five or six of us elder children and go out into the playground, and she'd explain the stars – Mars and Jupiter and that, and then we had to write about that the next day, and I know we always used to get a cup of cocoa and a bun before we came home. But still it was all education, wasn't it?

The real climax was when Tom Higdon dared to put himself up as candidate for the Parish Council elections of 1913. And more, had the impertinence to romp home on top of the poll. This was a heresy, since the local parson, the Rev. Eland, was supposed to be elected by divine right. He was also a School Manager. He was after the Higdons now.

MARJORIE LING The parson in the village said that she was wasting the coal to dry the children's clothes, you see, and of course he made it his business to try and get them out.

VIOLET POTTER The real reason why they got the sack was they were Labour people. Starting the Labourers Union, trying to improve the conditions. Footpaths round the village and toilets and different things for the poor old people who lived in these old houses belonging to the farms. That was the real reason.

The village believed in the Higdons; there were few friends elsewhere. The National Union of Teachers was very half-hearted. The Higdons had only the children.

MARJORIE LING The schoolmistress said: 'Now children,' she said, 'We're not allowed to teach any more in this school.'

VIOLET POTTER Our parents said: 'We're not going to let this rest.' And we had a meeting on the Green.

Well, I said to the children: 'We want to know who's going out on strike and who isn't.' All but about six said that they would come out. I think it was about 72 children went to school then and I put the names down on a sheet of paper. That night when Mr & Mrs Higdon finished up, we stayed behind and helped to take her possessions indoors, because she'd got her sewing machine and her camera and her typewriter and a lot of personal belongings in the school – in the council school and we took them into the schoolhouse.

The next day, 1 April 1914, everybody gathered at the village green. Only eight or nine children went to school. Everyone else was on strike.

MAY WILBY We all had pieces of cardboard, probably bits of bootbox or something like that, wrote on 'We want our teachers back'; 'We want justice'. Jack Mullinger had an accordion and we walked round the village. And as we walked past the school the mistress and the master were standing outside and she waved; I could see that she was crying.

VIOLET POTTER A police sergeant stood by and one or two of the church-wardens, they'd evidently got an inkling that something was going to happen and, of course, we went by singing with a piano-accordion playing 'Hearts of Oak' – dear, (laughs) that was our song. The main thing is, we knew from our parents that we were doing something what was just. I think every reason – big cause.

MAJORIE LING We sat all round the green and the woman at the village shop, she brought out pails of lemonade for us to drink. We were very hot. I always remember that 1 April.

From that 1 April the children's strike was almost 100 per cent. Annie and Tom Higdon had become folk-heroes, more famous every day. They gave up their school, but they did not surrender their vocation. Every day they held their classes in the open air of Burston Green.

But of course the law came in. Parents were sent to court for not sending their children to the official school. Collections were raised to pay the fines. But no one broke the strike.

And then one day someone offered the Higdons an old carpenter's shop in Burston to use as their own school.

MAJORIE LING There was a ladder went upstairs, but for the seniors; the little tots weren't allowed to go up that ladder. Always put me in mind of going up on board ship or something or other. It was rough in there but Mrs Higdon made it very, very comfortable for the children.

VIOLET POTTER We had a timetable like we had in the Council School, everything was worked to, you know, to time; starting from nine. Religious scriptures, and then arithmetic; eleven, playtime, which, of course, we had to use the Green for a playground.

The Inspectors came down two or three times to see if they could find any fault with the education, they couldn't find a bit of fault. I think they said the reading and writing was 'Well above the average, and the religion is taught on sensible lines'.

The feelings against the Parson, the Rev. Eland, had practically emptied his church. Services were now held in the open air by lay preachers and political radicals of all kinds. Burston became a place of pilgrimage for Trade Unions, led by the old socialist notables – Ben Tillet, Tom Mann, George Lansbury, Philip Snowden, and the great Suffragette family of the Pankhursts.

The Labour Movement seemed to find a symbol in this unknown East Anglian village, and funds came from everywhere for Annie Higdon.

VIOLET POTTER 'Some of the bigger girls,' she said, 'now you can open the mail.' Well, there would be paper-knives splitting open these – 'Oh I got a cheque for £5'. 'I got a cheque for £20.' There was one that was only half-a-crown and I think it was from an old-age pensioner. I shan't ever forget that because I said 'Whatever good is half-a-crown'. Mrs Higdon said 'Every little helps'. (laughs)

So, at last, Mr and Mrs Higdon's gesture of independence achieved the solid form of a new and tangible Strike School of their own, paid for by supporters everywhere who may never have clapped eyes on Burston, but who knew what it meant. And on 13 May 1917, while the Great War raged, the Burston Strike School was opened, and there the invincible Higdons taught their village children for more than twenty years.

TOM POTTER To my mind we got a socialist education. For example, if we had what we called a bible lesson, well then usually it turned round to the way that Christ sided always with the working class against the property owners and the church at the time.

WYN POTTER We'd start at school with a hymn. But they were different hymns, not the ordinary kind, you know, like:

'When wilt Thou save Thy people?
Oh God of mercy, when?
The people Lord, the people;
Not thrones and crowns but men?'

TOM POTTER Farm workers wages were twenty-five to thirty shillings a week at that time. Mrs Higdon did actually pay my parents in order that I could keep at school. Not being a recognised school, we were not allowed to enter for the grammar school exam, so I never got the chance to go to the secondary school but she did pay my parents I believe ten bob a week, so that I could stay on at school another year, and this I did.

WYN POTTER My mother and father always declared that I was not going to domestic service, that was the customary thing for girls in the village. Not if they had to work and keep me, they were not going to let me do that but, anyway, they didn't have to because when I got to the strike school Mrs Higdon suggested that I should learn shorthand and typing and she presented me with the books and the typewriter and I got going.

By the mid 1930s there were still about 20 Burston children going to Annie Higdon's school, still being taught the truth as she saw it, not as she was told to see it, still stubbornly refusing all help. The Higdons were not going to surrender any hold on their achievement. But they, like it, could not last forever.

In August 1939 – twenty-five years after the Burston children, now long grown up, had come out on their famous strike – Tom

Higdon died. From all over the country Trade Union leaders came to his burial – in Burston graveyard, so the Church got that tough old dissident at last.

His wife Annie carried on the school for a while before she joined him.

The famous Strike School remains – but it is no longer a school but a village hall. Or, perhaps, a monument.

The Levant Mine Disaster

Drawing by R. L. Ellis of the man engine

Away down at the edge of England near Land's End, where Cornwall slides into the sea, is the village of St Just. They used to say for generations that nothing mattered to Cornishmen but music, Methodism, and mining. There are not many miners left in St Just today.

Three miles down the coast from St Just was once the tin-mine of Levant. It was the largest and the richest; they dug their tin from levels 2000 feet deep stretching a mile below the sea. That is, until the disaster over half a century ago. It was in the year 1919.

It was the St Just men dug the tin from the Levant. It was hot and hard, and dangerous and dirty. Around the turn of the century the management built them a changing-room.

BOB PROWSE Oh, it was a most beautiful building. There was about I should say four hundred in here at least. It was a changing room. We used to call it the 'dry'. And this is where the men used to come up from underground, all wet. And then we'd make a dive for this. We were maybe twenty in that little pond there, and twenty in that one. And one or two round the basins with their legs up. Couldn't get mine up there now. (laughs)

Missus used to say: 'Don't you wash your back,' when we'd been home for a night or two. 'No don't wash your back'; wasn't allowed to wash your backs, that made your back weak.

There was a strange archaic machine that took them down to the deep workings: it was called the Man-Engine. It was a great rod, driven by a Cornish beam-engine, and not a photograph of it still exists. The principle was a simple series of steps, twelve feet apart, spaced out down the great main rod. Each man stuck his candle on his tull, which was his hat, travelled down on his step to the next platform, and waited till the man-engine rod returned. One hundred and thirty miners could make the same descent on the half-hour journey. Before the man-engine, a hundred years before, they had had to climb both ways by ladder – maybe an hour and a half to make the surface. They blessed the man-engine. Lionel Ellis went to Levant Mine in 1912 and drove this machine for seven years.

LIONEL ELLIS I was just the engine driver, that's all. I had a stoker there, of course, because I wasn't allowed to leave the engine. Well, the engine would start at half past six in the morning regular as clockwork. And each man would come down, get on to the step which would then be lowered level with the sollar, and that would drop down the 12 feet. Every 12 feet there was a step about two foot square, and about three foot six to four foot six up there was a handle for you to catch hold of.

ALBERT DYMOND Really it was as safe as anything, a child could ride on it. I started with a man being brought down with me, two on a step. After three days, well you got on all right. You had to take a candle in your hat and a lantern in your hand, for a while. But after that you put the lantern one side and just used the candle.

Tin was a great traditional job down there in St Just. The lads followed their fathers, their uncles, their brothers down the big hole. Mines, Methodism, and music; they all came together there in Cornwall.

WILLIAM LAWRY They had four male voice choirs in this district. Most of the men worked in the mine. When they travelled the man-engine they all started to sing, and the sound that you heard as it came up through the shaft was out of this world. If you could stand on top of that shaft and listen – rich it was, rich. Some never used to believe in church and chapels or anything like that, but they would join in the hymns, you know, and everybody's heart and soul in it.

But the man-engine was not what it was; it was getting old and full of years. By 1919 it was said to be the last one working in the world. The miners began to worry about it, and many packed up the job. Even the driver grew nervous, and finally *he* turned it in.

LIONEL ELLIS It was because I could hear this thump and thump every now and then; that shouldn't be. That was the shaftman's duty, but the manager was a sick man. He wouldn't spend much time up with me anyway. Nobody spent much time with me. I was generally alone. Well, this constant groaning I got frightened about, so I told the chief engineer, if you can't put me on another engine I'm shifting altogether. I aren't stopping here no longer. All right, he said, I'll give you a job at the Higher Bell that's a little mine further up. And two weeks after that the accident happened.

MRS WILLIAM MURLEY I heard them talking a few weeks before the accident, my husband and two of his underground friends, and they were discussing about the man-engine then. And I heard them saying that it was making a lot of creaking noise which they didn't like. So they thought that it should have been seen into. But I don't think it ever was. It did happen. And it cost the mine all those men's lives. My husband was twenty-nine.

We got up at about six every morning and he used to have a cooked breakfast and then I would pack his lunch for him and by about half past six he would leave for work. Go away quite happy seeming, they would be. In the mornings of course at that time in the mornings it's lovely and fresh, you see.

That Monday, 20 October 1919, Mrs Murley, seven months pregnant with her third, saw William off as usual.

MRS MURLEY Well, he was gone about five minutes and I heard him running back and he came back for his matchbox – a box they used underground, a brass to keep the matches dry, you see, and the little boy had it playing with on Sunday and it was gone in under the chair, and he forgot all about it and he came back for it. We used to say that was quite a bad omen for them to come back like that.

LIONEL ELLIS I was five minutes walk from the mine and I suddenly saw the half of the wheel collapse. Well, I knew what had happened, but the manager and the captain were down in the stoke hole preparing for a new boiler. When I told them, they went white as death, they both of them, they knew what had happened better than I did then.

What they knew was that the great man-engine rod had collapsed. And with it, the men. Albert Dymond had just come off it.

ALBERT DYMOND I was gone up into the dry, about to change, get in the bath. Suddenly they shouted 'Man-engine has stopped'. Looked out through the window; it had stopped all right, something had gone wrong. Nobody coming up. At last up came Mr Carbis, 'My God', he said, 'man-engine's broken. There's some slaughter down there, here's some damage done.' Right, we went back now and looked – all open shaft.

JOHN JAMES I was about to step in, and she made a quiver, you know, and I dodged back and under. And that was that, down she goes. Of course what happened, see, the main pin on the top broke, see. And then the rod on the way down broke in half. That's what done the damage. That went right through see, down to the 60 level, took everything with it.

MRS MURLEY Had my two children in bed with the measles at the time and I got around quickly and did finish the washing. Waiting for my husband to come, got his dinner all under hand for him – and was there waiting from three till half past three expecting him, you know, and of course it went on till four o'clock, half past four, he didn't come. Well, I thought they might have had something broke underground and they had to walk up, which would make them later, so of course I lingered around wondering. And of course as the time went on it comes to five o'clock, six o'clock and I still had no news of anything. By that time I thought there was something happened, and of course one or two of the neighbours came in then and I said to them, I think there's been an accident. Well, they wanted to keep it from me if they could, but I was convinced it was something wrong. Then the neighbours sent for my parents to come down. And they came there and stayed with me all the night and another neighbour, and of course, I knew by that time that there was something wrong. Of course I had no official news, but I knew then – because I heard them saying there was such a lot of men who hadn't returned home.

It was once again the endless story of the miners' wives, who wait for men who will not return. The wives went over to Levant, and waited in the dry, where the men used to bath and change. They could hear men calling up from the shaft for ropes, and ladders, and help. Almost everyone volunteered.

ALBERT DYMOND I said 'I'll go'. 'Oh no, you're too young. 'I'll go,' I said, so I got on the ladder. 'Now,' he said, 'when you get down the bottom, be careful' he said, 'because you might step off and go further'. I went down the ladder, quietly, and I got to the last stave and I looked – oh, it might have been about six or eight foot down. And there it was, the whole shaft come together. And I could see them lying down, no movement, presumed they were dead. Afterwards I found out that they picked up four or five from there that was dead.

BOB PROWSE The ladders were swinging forth and back and it was very dangerous. A moan came from a man in front of me, and there was a little piece of a ladder there. I made a grip on the ladder to save myself. I was a bunch of nerves, believe me. And there he was, with all the slush and everything running from the shaft down his face and mouth. And he was pinned by his right hand and knee to the wall of the shaft one side, and the left hand outstretched and jammed that side. He started to moan and groan again, so what I done was put some timber there that took away the water that was running in his face and chest. And he – well, he like, like closed up then, went quiet, so I guessed that I'd done something for him, poor fellow. He was picked up about five o'clock in the morning, he died later.

Young Willie Lawry had started work underground only three weeks earlier.

WILLIAM LAWRY I was two steps above what we call 80, that's 80 fathoms. I was two steps above that when the engine broke away. And I was dug out two steps below that, a matter of 48 feet. Now the man that I worked with, he was a step below me, and he was found down 10. And the man above me, a man called Willy Waters, he was dug out before they found me, and he was dead. So actually I was very fortunate. I had 36 stitches in my face and neck, lost all my front teeth, a collar bone broken and 8 ribs crushed. Took me 12 months before I started to work again.

JOHN JAMES We were stretcher bearers, you know. Started to take them back, one down and one up the next stage, and we got they two back. I don't know, about hour and a half I suppose, and then we got sent from there up to 60th level, went up there and brought three or four more back, dead. Then we were sent from there up to 24 level. I was afternoon shift, I went down two o'clock and never went home no more until eight o'clock next evening. Twelve we carried out there. And two of them was our neighbours here. Yes, funerals here, funerals there, for days and days and days.

Thirty-one men died in the Levant that day. The people of St Just and Pendeen were angry, bewildered and bitter. When the mine officials appeared publicly they were abused, and even called murderers. Rightly or wrongly, the villagers believed that the man-engine had been overworked, because the mine-owners merely wanted to get out the tin and had not had time to inspect the machine properly.

At the offical enquiry the verdict was: an accident caused by fatigue of a defective part of the man-engine.

ALBERT DYMOND Quite a number of them was asked into the enquiry, but Will Ellis nor me was never asked. So someone said, how don't you go to the enquiry? Will said, 'If I go I shall tell the truth. I shall tell the truth if I go'. He was never asked, nor was I.

Everyone around Cornwall and the West Country gave what they could to the Levant Mine Disaster Fund. It was divided very arbitrarily. If anyone had a pension, they deducted any Fund compensation you got.

WILLIAM LAWRY I wasn't more than fourteen and six weeks, you see. So I wasn't entitled to anything from the National Health or Industrial Injuries. And father was too quiet, he didn't intercede in regard to the Levant Disaster Fund.

MRS MURLEY We were eleven months before we got any compensation. And then a member of parliament from Plymouth, Sir Isaac Foot, fought for it, and he got it. I don't think the mine intended to pay it. They didn't seem as if they wanted to. Of course it was a very big thing – there were 31, you see, poor men. When the children were growing up, it was very short. Of course they allowed you what they called a 'living', but then as your children got bigger they needed more food and they needed bigger clothes and boots. We could have done with some extra money. I went out to wash two days a week. I hear now they've got many many thousands that will never be spent.

For the last three Christmasses they've given us a £5 note, a little extra over the Christmas. Well I could have done with that when the children were small, it would have been very welcome.

Cornwall is studded with the decaying workings of discarded tin-mines, and the shades of forgotten miners. The Levant Mine at St Just, where the man-engine failed, has never worked again.

The Victorian Girls

Frances E. Jones

The first of the women's freedom fighters lived long before the Lib Ladies of our day, before the Suffragettes of yesterday, before the century was born. They were the Victorian Girls. They did not really fight for freedom, they fought for fun. Indeed they did not seriously fight for anything, they worked for it, in an age when gentlewomen rarely worked for anything.

Two of the Old Victorian Girls met together not very long ago to talk together of the days of their youth, of lavender and old lace, of the Typewriting Machine and The Growler, of the Little Coteries and the Drawing-Room Ballads – and of the strangely hard work in between. No comment is necessary. These two old professional ladies – well into their nineties – by their memories alone leave a whiff of a graceful and far from pompous age; their wit and observation make them the best of Period Pieces.

Miss Frances E. Jones, whom her friends knew as 'F. E. Jones', was one of the very first of the Victorian women to be trained as a shorthand typist. That was in 1892, when the woman's world was just beginning to open up.

Miss Berta Ruck, another emergent lady of the 1890s, was originally an art-student, but her long life's work turned into the writing of romantic novels. She published well over a hundred books.

MISS RUCK In those days, you see, we lived under the slogan 'Of Course'. We never imagined that anything would ever be different. Of Course we went to Church, Of Course people got married if they possibly could, Of Course certain classes went and were presented at Buckingham Palace to Queen Victoria. Of Course this, Of Course that.

When I was born my father was away in Afghanistan where he was supposed to be holding a fort. It could nowadays have been wiped out with one bomb. But then, my father doesn't seem to have done anything but just knit his socks.

MISS JONES I was born in Westminster in August 1875, I was my parents' ninth child. My father looked at me and said: 'Dear, dear, *that* won't live'.

I was a very weedy, skinny, anaemic child, and always what boys called a grizzle-guts. That went on until I was near seventeen. Then one day my brother said he'd been down Victoria Street, and he had looked in a great big shop window there and there they had some sort of little machine and some ladies were working this machine, and he understood they were called typewriters, and it said in the window 'Students Taken'. So I went round one morning. And this very nice owner interviewed me, and said what did I want to do? and I said I'd like to come and see if I could learn to do this typing. I'd only been there about four or five months and I got on the staff for this big sum of eight shillings a week. After a time some of the offices started having typewriters and engaging girls as clerks.

MISS RUCK I was at a girls school in North Wales. The headmistress had me up and said: 'You are an indolent and feckless girl. You are drawing in your exercise book when you ought to be concentrating on your work, because child, what are we put into this world for?' I looked at her and said: 'Sometimes I don't think any of us know'. She looked at me and said: 'To prepare, dear, prepare for what we are going to do'.

And of course I didn't know what I was going to do. I went on being a feckless and indolent girl, and presently when I left school, my father said: 'I don't know what we shall do with Berta. She wouldn't be any use at anything but drawing. She had better go somewhere they talk about drawing all the time, she'd better go to London'. So I went. Finished up at the Slade.

Mud everywhere. Hansom cabs slurring through the mud, and where there wasn't mud there was fog, and in between was us, enjoying ourselves.

I do remember the buses of that time. The great thing was to get in front by the driver, where you had a lovely view of the street and everything as you went by. Everybody wore hats of course, and those profuse underclothes which were still the go, they wore long skirts that had to be held up out of the mud. When I think of the hours we spent brushing our skirts. Of course they had underneath a dreadful thing called – what was it? It was the braid under the skirt which was a sort of horse hair and it was supposed to take up all the mud, but it didn't. The sort of time that nowadays is spent looking at the telly, we spent brushing our skirts and darning our stockings. Because we had woollen stockings that used to wear into holes, and those we had to darn. Hours we spent.

At ten o'clock, by which time I was in bed and my gas was out, I used to hear 'Time Gentlemen. Time now,' and out would stream cockneys who had been enjoying themselves, do you see, until they were outed, and they used to come along the gutter, some of them holding the others up, and singing songs which are embedded in my memory. Do you think I might dare to sing one of them now?

She may have known better days
When she was in her prime.
She may have known better days
Once upon a time.
When by the roadside she fell,
Oh never pass her by,
Some poor old mother is waiting for her,
Who has known better days.

MISS JONES You could get a pint of porter for three ha'pence, but if you had a glass of brandy or anything like that, that was a bit dearer. I do remember they used to say that they got quite a good glass of gin for tuppence ha'penny.

There were some very poor streets near Westminster Abbey, and a soup kitchen in York Street, and they used to come down with bowls in the winter. They'd go in there with these bowls and they'd get a great big bowl of soup and a chunk of bread for a penny. There was a very great deal of poverty.

MISS RUCK No doubt we did think: oh my God, this is awful. We didn't say so, we never protested. Of Course, people worked in factories for about two shillings a day, if that. Of Course people all wore hats in the street. Of Course people called each other Miss and Mister until they were engaged. Of Course there was no such thing as – as anything but Of Course.

In the early 90s very few offices had typewriting machines of their own. Miss Jones's agency was one of only about half a dozen in London.

MISS JONES A young medical student from St Thomas' Hospital used to come along and bring little scripts, little stories. His name was Somerset Maugham, and he had written a book called 'Liza of Lambeth', then people began to take him up. So he used to bring the little scripts to us, little stories to type for him.

We used to go out to different offices, but if we went a long distance we used to take the typewriter on what used to be called 'growlers' – the old fourwheelers. We had to cart it along and get it out of the four-wheeler, and sometimes the man was kind and would help you out with it. But sometimes we had to lift this rather heavy machine.

I went one day to Park Lane to type some letters for the Honourable George Wyndham, who was then the Governor General of Ireland. They'd a very cheeky young footman there, and he was not going to lift the machine for me. The kind man who'd been on the four-wheeler put it on the step, but the young footman looked at me with great disgust – fancy a young girl coming to work for a man. And he left the machine on the ground. I was about 18 or 19.

When the lady came downstairs and she saw this young man letting a young girl try to pick up this machine, she called out 'John, pick up that machine and take it into your master's study'. So he had to. Then she said 'Would you like a cup of tea?' I've always remembered it.

I went to work for a missionary one day who lived in Bloomsbury. I had a cold and I blew my nose. And she said 'Don't forget I'm paying half a crown an hour.'

MISS RUCK In my art-student days, the thing to be was decadent, which meant you liked The Yellow Book, and that you liked all the drawings of Aubrey Beardsley, and you liked the poem by Oscar Wilde, 'The Sphinx'.

> From a dim corner of my room,
> For longer than my fancy thinks,
> A beautiful and silent sphinx
> Hath watched me through the gathering gloom.

That we thought was perfect. Well, it was quite good.

We talked about the theatre, we talked about each other, but I tell you what we didn't talk about, we didn't talk about politics. We knew something of the sort was going on, but we were enjoying ourselves in our little coteries. Everything was either 'ripping' or 'foul' or 'rotten'. The girls didn't smoke, the boys used to drink beer, but we didn't drink except at dances when we used to have what we thought was most doggish of us – claret cup.

MISS JONES Well, I won't tell you his name, but he was a well-known Member of Parliament for some place in Ireland, and I went with him one night to dinner at the Café Royal. We had velvet cushions for seats; I believe it was like that up to a few years ago. And they brought a great sort of cockadoodle thing, put it on the table after we'd had dinner. And I looked at it, and the friend who was giving me dinner said 'Oh, it's all right, lift it up'. There was a lovely ice cream inside it, a great big bombe, like. So I had a jolly good tuck-in, and then I went back and did some work. And you know we never quarrelled about going out in the evenings, and we never charged any extra, and I never got any overtime.

Bicycles had come in by now. So after a time, after saving up some of my eight shillingses, I was able to have a bicycle. And then came the question about dress. Well, there was a woman who used to go round Bloomsbury in some very voluminous things, called bloomers. But when our dress came in, we called it Rational Dress. You had a flapping thing down that lapped right down to your knees, and then when you went home you took it off and folded it on the back of the bicycle, and put your skirts on, because it would never do for the neighbours to see you in what was called a very very indecent dress. We used to do quite long drives. We had cushion tyres in those days. We'd go down on a Saturday afternoon as far as Brighton or Worthing and come back the next day.

One of our first office engagements was to the Automobile Club. It wasn't called Royal in those days, it was the Automobile Club. They were trying to get their first 300 members, and there was a very energetic secretary called Claude Johnson, who afterwards became the manager of Rolls Royce, and one day Claude Johnson took me up to Carlisle, because he wanted to start one of the first goings up and down the hills on a car. I don't know how old I was then, about twenty, but of course it was quite a wrong thing to do, for a young woman to be sent up with a man, up North. But well, I did it. The office was well-paid for it, and there was nothing about it, but just going on a job.

MISS RUCK A really well-bred society girl was scarcely ever without a chaperone.

MISS JONES If your people were anybody – for instance if you lived in Berkeley Square, or Belgrave Square, all that – the girls never went out without a maid. But I was only a very ordinary person, and by that time I had become almost what you might call a working person.

MISS RUCK I was very glad I was an art student. We did do things, and went about as well-bred girls, sheltered girls, never did. Once I even got as far as Paris. I was asked to this smart restaurant, and I didn't have a dress.

I went to a fellow student, a Welsh girl, she'd got the most wonderful fair hair with real gold tints in it. She afterwards married Keillers Marmalade, and her hair was exactly that colour, we used to think she'd done it on purpose.

Her name was Dolly Philmorris, she was very tall, my height then, and I was almost as slim as she was, and so she said: 'Well, Rucky dear, here is this black frock dear, you can wear this to go out with your fate in'. That was another thing, we used to call these young men our fate.

My escort who was very rich, he said, 'I've been to an auction sale today,' and he'd paid a lot for a pair of garters. He said they were made of woven silver and the buckles were real emeralds in the shape of hearts. He said they fetched I don't know how many thousand francs a pair, and I said in my innocence: 'Fancy giving all that money for things that would never be seen again'. And he looked at me and said: 'Whoever gave that present would see it again'. I didn't know what he meant. You can imagine.

Through the art school crowd I met a lot of writers – H. G. Wells, and the Chestertons, the fat one and the other one, and G. B. Shaw. H. G. Wells was a great disappointment. He was a little pink-faced man with a squeaky little voice. He said to me 'Go back, Aristocracy, to your mountains, you don't belong here'. And I was very hurt at this, but however afterwards he became a great friend. And you realised that through this very unprepossessing exterior was a great man; women used to run after him. That I don't understand. I've always liked people to be rather more decorative.

MISS JONES I went to do some work for Sir Ernest Hart, the Editor of the British Medical Journal. I was typing some dictation from him, and he said 'Would you like to have the fire? Well, just put a match to it.' I went over to light up the fire, and I struck a match as we did at home, on the mantelpiece. He was very cross . . . 'Don't you know that's a Grinling Gibbons?' Well, I'd no idea what a Grinling Gibbons was, but still I knew I was in trouble. But afterwards he did send word to the office to say I was a very good speller.

I think the young women of today should be grateful for all things that we older ones did, because we pushed open the door a little bit, and we opened the life for the younger woman.

MISS RUCK I think the late Victorians really used to wallow in sentimentality. The Queen I think started it, she was really quite sentimental in this way. She didn't worry about children in factories, she was as sheltered as many of her subjects.

But her funeral in 1901 was a very splendid affair. The music was Chopin's funeral march – she didn't want the Dead March from Saul, she left orders. Then came the little tiny coffin with the Union Jack on it, and people saying: 'She must have been a very little lady,' and people saying 'Five Kings to follow her', amongst whom was the German Kaiser.

It was never the same again – we who'd believed it was going to be always as it was, under the phrase 'Of Course', believed there would be always the same sort of Royal Family, the same British Empire, it was never to be the same again. Then came the War – the First War. Bang! Everything changed, it was never the same. It was never 'Of Course'.

The Battle of Cable Street

Police chasing demonstrators, 4 October 1936

On the fourth of October 1936, a part of East London not far from Aldgate became a battlefield. Nothing like it had been seen before. For this was the day the British Fascists attempted to March through the Jewish East End, and when a quarter of a million Londoners mobilised to prevent them. It became known in days to come as The Battle of Cable Street.

Cable Street was London at its poorest and most vulnerable. One man planned to bring to this bleak place the harsh and alien message of Fascism. His name was Sir Oswald Mosley – and this name still echoes through his old haunts.

FIRST MAN IN PUB Shall I tell you something . . . Mosley's theme and policy was England for the English. Am I right? He'd have thrown out the

Jews, he'd have thrown out the coloureds, he'd have thrown out everybody else, and I tell you who'd have been left here – Mosley, Northcliffe, Rothermere, Leverhulme, the lot; they'd have had what was left. And I'll tell you where you would have been – in the gutter.

SECOND MAN IN PUB There's no justification in calling Mosley a saviour. Mosley's a nothing, he's a nobody. He just used the political situation at the time to further his own ends at the expense of the Jews of East London.

THIRD MAN IN PUB Give him a proper answer, a murderer, like all Fascists are murderers. That's the right answer, a truthful answer.

Fascism was a terribly meaningful thing in the 30s. It loomed over Europe like a stormcloud. And its apostle in Britain was Sir Oswald Mosley – who even forty years on in his self-imposed exile, had never given up.

OSWALD MOSLEY Really, these strange events – as they must be to this generation – of long ago should be studied in their background. That is what is really important about it. Why were we there, what were we doing. Sometimes it's said we wanted to impose ourselves in some way on the people of East London. That's quite untrue. Our vote in East London the following March after these events was 23% in Bethnal Green and 19% in Limehouse. And that was an old people's vote. Householders only had the vote in the LCC elections. Young people who were with us at that time had no vote, and in a parliamentary election we should clearly have won. But a large and organised crowd from far afield, little to do with East London, were brought there to stop us doing what we had often done before, to have a propaganda march through East London.

Cable Street was one of the punctuation marks of our times, for it was there that the Londoners looked Fascism in the eye, and said No. Oswald Mosley had been England's most brilliant misfit. He was rich and clever and one of the white hopes of the Labour Party – until he looked across the Channel and found new models in two men, called Benito Mussolini and Adolf Hitler.

If Fascism could succeed in Italy and Germany, why not in Britain? That was what Mosley put to the nation.

MOSLEY (1930s newsreel) Fascism is new to Great Britain. Because it is new it will be attacked by some and laughed at by others. Fools always laugh at what they do not understand.

Indeed the concept of Fascism was new – at least in London. Fascism was patriotism perverted into power; it was law-and-order corrupted into tyranny; it believed that only Authority was needed to control a nation's thought for its own good. There were many, in those depressed days who feared trouble from the hungry and frustrated and unemployed, and who said that discipline was the only answer. Mosley's movement, the Blackshirts, became the British Union of Fascists, and it was not short of rich support. Lord Nuffield gave a cheque for £50,000. Lord Rothermere bestowed the backing of his *Daily Mail.*

But by and by Mosley lost the patronage of the *Daily Mail.* He would not dissociate his movement from Hitler and the methods of the Nazis. Jewish firms withdrew their advertising from the *Mail,* and the *Mail* withdrew its sponsorship of Mosley. The Blackshirts, outside the political mainstream, took to the streets in uniform.

OSWALD MOSLEY I was of course myself a soldier, as you probably know, in the first war. And half of me reverted to my being a professional soldier. I have admitted publicly that the old soldier rather got the better of the politician when I allowed to be worn a very military uniform. We began with an ordinary black shirt and then we developed full military uniform because soldiers, which we had then become, do like a smart uniform.

And Mosley's soldiers moved in where the ground was fertile, as they thought – into the dim and dispossessed region of the docks and the slums.

BILL FISHMAN For months on end our fathers were in the dole queue, walking the streets, seeking work, food was scarce, there was a feeling of despair and frustration. There was a common sentiment, common experience to all peoples of East London, and above all there was the eternal slums, the litter, the dirt, the filth, the futility of it all.

One man argued that he could bring purpose and order to the demoralised East End – Mosley, with his political melodrama.

MOSLEY (1930s recording) . . . And the lives of great nations, comes the moment of decision, comes the moment of destiny. And this Nation again and again in the great hours of its faith has swept aside convention, has swept aside the little men, a token of delay, has decided to follow men and movements who dare, who go forward to action. They who dare follow us in this hour. Theirs is the mighty mood of Britain.

BILL FISHMAN It is very easy in a time of economic crisis to turn to a scapegoat and in East London the scapegoat was evident, the Jews. There was still an alien community, a pretty defenceless minority.

The Blackshirts held regular street meetings in East London. I remember them well. I used to stand at the back of the crowd, probably as much out of cowardice as anything else. In the front were the masses of these blackshirted warriors and a van would draw up and then on top of the van a bright light would shine on the leader himself; one could hear the chanting M.O.S.L.E.Y., we want Mosley. At that time it used to hit me right in the guts because Mosley to me personified all that was evil in my experience. He got up, I can see him now, very handsome, very dignified, and he came over not like his fellow dictators in Europe with the rancour and ranting. He was rational in his argument, and he reached his crescendo very slowly, and when he did, up would jump the front line of men shouting 'Hail Mosley!' and one could hear also 'Perish, Judah, down with the Jews.'

Someone who was not a Jew was aware of all this, who taught for years in a college in the heart of the East End: Edith Ramsey.

EDITH RAMSEY Indeed Mosley did have a measure of success. Before his activities relationships throughout the whole district were very easy. Well, we took Jewish differences for granted and they took our differences for granted. After Mosley, one became very conscious one was speaking to a Jew, and the Jews were, I think, very naturally on the outlook for signs of disapproval or anti-semitism, and detected them in the minds of their most ardent well-wishers. It became not a normal relationship. That was what Mosley did.

OSWALD MOSLEY The Jew is not, I think the Jews will agree, immune from criticism. That is, if a Jew does something wrong then he is liable to be criticised as you or I. Actually, to take ourselves back to that period, prior to the war, the position was more normal. Since the war I, like many other people have been particularly sensitive to that question, because the Jews were so terribly vilely treated in Germany, which I and everyone else has condemned. But at that time they were in a normal position, and if a Jew were shouting for war as we thought, he would be attacked.

BILL FISHMAN We were constantly in a state of tension, particularly in Stepney and Bethnal Green. We already had news of what was going on in Germany and here at first hand we were feeling the impact of a similar sort of experience.

EDITH RAMSEY There was the terrible occasion when a Jewish girl was caught in White Horse Lane and was strapped to some hoarding in the attitude of the crucifiction. A girl of 13, perhaps 12. And at their public meetings their gospel was, get rid of the Jews. Why is everything wrong, why weren't these people living in the houses they wanted? The Jews were living in them. Why didn't they have the jobs they wanted? The Jews had got them. Why did we keep the Jews in England when every civilised country in Europe was getting rid of them? The Jews were bribing our government.

BILL FISHMAN I often used to go away feeling 'Are we Jews like this?' Often when he used to call out about international finance, the alien domination of British politics, my mind used to go to my own father, who was a poor tailor wandering through the East End looking for work. How could one equate this with those international alien financiers who were eroding Britain, according to Sir Oswald Mosley?

News of the coming October Blackshirt March on Stepney had reached the East End in advance, and a growing mass of opposition was mobilised by the Communists. One of the leaders of the resistance was Phil Piratin, who was later to go to Westminster as a Communist MP.

PHIL PIRATIN One of the things we were concerned to know about was the movement of the Fascists. For this purpose we called together a number of people as observers, some people would call them spies. We gathered about two dozen young people, all of them looking as Aryan as we could find them. They all seemed suitably enough Aryan-looking, except for one who I then knew as Mr Faulkner. I said he had better stop out as he could look Jewish. He said: 'I am not Jewish, I am of Irish descent.' I said, but you look Jewish.

HUGH FAULKNER He said 'You look more of a bloody yid than I do . . .'

PHIL PIRATIN I don't think I said that, never mind, if you say so. When he mentioned he was a doctor I realised how valuable that would be.

In Cable Street I saw the way they were stacking up the barricades with mattresses, and the way these dockers and labourer types were working alongside the bearded Jews. Now I had already lived in Stepney all my life, and I was then 29, and I had never seen this before.

HUGH FAULKNER Before the actual day I got my best suit, borrowed a hat, we used to call Anthony Eden hats in those days, a black hat. Borrowed a little black case. When I got to the place I was asked to go and observe, I found a solid line of police. So I said 'Doctor' very firmly, and got through one line of police, and then another. And I found myself right in the middle of the Mosley fascists. And just by sheer luck I happened to catch sight of a member of the Mosley fascists who was at my hospital, who was a very notorious character. On the spur of the moment I said: 'I've finally made up my mind, I want to come in with you,' and although I was secretary of the Socialist Society in the hospital and never concealed it, he was such a clot that he immediately accepted that on this one day I had suddenly decided to change my way of life, and was absolutely delighted. He was very proud of me. Almost immediately I was shown a duplicated plan of the route. Well, I could hardly believe all this, and said: 'Well if I'm going to stop I had better go and move my car'. So I went out with my little bag and my hat, through the three lines of police. I rang up the number I had been told and said I had just seen the plan of the march. I was met with complete incredulity at the other end. The voice obviously didn't believe a word of it, and I was almost in tears trying to explain that I really had seen the plan.

PHIL PIRATIN Our main objective was to prevent the fascists marching either along Whitechapel Road or along Commercial Road, where most of the Jewish people were congregated and where the greatest provocation could have been caused.

BILL FISHMAN I was about 15 at the time. The whole of this main thoroughfare was crowded, one could hardly get in between one person and another. And there was a forest of banners, and one stands out in my mind. 'They Shall Not Pass.' I remember, though I didn't really understand, that this is why I had come out with my fellow Jews, that the fascists would not pass in East London.

EDITH RAMSEY I was trying to get through because I was going to a Sunday School. And there in the courtyard of Brunswick Buildings, sitting on an old box was an old Jewish woman with her wig all askew – you know that the Jews have to shave when they marry not to attract other men – we had many of those immigrant Jews in their wigs in those days – swaying backwards and forwards moaning. And I said 'Oh Granny, granny, it is all right. It can't happen. Don't worry.' And she said to me 'Oh lady, lady, I have seen it in Poland. It is coming here'. And you knew the dread of that age-long persecution which is the blackest blot on the history of Christendom was in her mind, as indeed in some ways it is and must be in the minds of every Jew.

PHIL PIRATIN When more people came along we directed them down Leman Street so that at one stage this was also blocked. We gave little attention to the Highway because we felt in no circumstances would he march in that direction. The police tried again and again to break the blockage here. They couldn't break through because the crowd was so dense.

By now in the East End there were something like a quarter of a million people confronting the police.

PHIL PIRATIN The police were working in very difficult circumstances, and without a doubt the rank and file police were carrying out their instructions, but they were as vicious as anything I have ever seen, including some of the hunger marches. On this occasion they were attacking the local people, including women and children.

Outside the Mint the Blackshirts heard that the Police had not been able to beat a path for them through this multitude, and decided to change their plan. Hugh Faulkner, the agent in their midst, passed on the news.

PHIL PIRATIN And so when they began to try and get through here we had a barricade at this junction. This is where we had prepared to overturn a lorry which had been given to us by a local lorry firm for overturning purposes. And we were going to overturn this, and the instructions were to set it alight. In fact, the chaps in charge here took the wrong lorry, the ignition key must have been inside, they turned it over. They also forgot to put it alight. Nevertheless that lorry plus other things which we had in the way, prevented the police coming further. When the police broke through here on the first barricade they met with an opposition here which in fact was even a surprise to us. It was along this street, Cable Street, that from the roofs and the upper floors people, ordinary housewives, elderly women were throwing down milk bottles and all kinds of refuse on to the police.

The Battle of Cable Street is known for this reason: it was there that the police really had to fight for themselves, not for the Fascists.It was at that point that the police threw down their batons; that one or two police actually surrendered. The local people – mostly they were dockers living around there in those days – took their helmets and their batons as souvenirs for their children.

Back near the Mint, Hugh Faulkner watched Sir Oswald Mosley go and talk to the Police Commissioner, Sir Philip Game.

HUGH FAULKNER Mosley was gesticulating, marching up and down with Sir Philip Game, who was clearly telling him that it was impossible to go on. It was quite clear that the people of the East End were not going to allow Mosley to march with his blackshirts through.

OSWALD MOSLEY We never clashed with this organised mob at all. We were halted by the police and told to disperse about half a mile away, and as usual we obeyed the police. So we were prevented doing what we had often done before, marching through East London in an area where we had this tremendous vote and would have certainly won a parliamentary election at that time.

Later Sir Oswald announced to the Press: 'This is the first time a British Government has surrendered to Red Terror'.

BILL FISHERMAN Oh there was absolute relief, there were parties, dancing in the streets, the cafés were full, pubs were full, and there was a feeling of elation, and feeling of relief, particularly amongst the immigrant Jews, because I think from that day onwards Mosley never again ventured into the ghetto streets of East London.

In almost any East End pub – and pubs all through the land – the argument goes on, the old racial debate of the 30s translated into the uneasy context of today. Yesterday's Witness is not so long ago, nor so far away.

MEN IN PUB There was only one thing made Moseley a great leader . . . what he spoke was true . . . what he spoke was right . . . Violence only came at the blackshirt meetings for the simple reason that all you were fighting for was a better standard of living and the type of people you represent . . .

We had a lot of aliens in the country at that time who had come from Russia, they were out to destroy his meetings wherever they could, thus preventing the British people from hearing a policy that would have saved this country.

I'm asking if you agree that Oswald Mosley's policy that England should be for the English . . .

No, no, here . . . let him answer it . . .

I don't care whether you listen to me, it don't make no difference to me . . .

He picked on the Jews at first, then he picked on the Irish because they were southern Irish, now all he could pick on was the spades.

Now, now, now, now . . . Don't talk like that. Don't mention colour . . . Who's talking about colour . . . We're talking about Mosley, he was a white man . . .

There wasn't much of a colour prejudice in Britain . . .

I don't care . . . I don't care . . .

The British Union of Fascists policy was England for the English . . .

Which is right . . .

But you're contradicting yourself.

I'm not contradicting myself . . .

In Petticoat Lane one Geoffrey Hamm, a Mosley man undismayed by a generation's history, still preaches the old Blackshirt message, and is not ignored.

GEOFFREY HAMM In the 1930s Britain had the greatest empire the world had ever seen, one that covered one quarter of the earth's surface, one that had one fifth of the world's population. If you had had good strong government, if you had had the right people at Westminster, that great wealth would have been developed in order to give our people the finest standard of living which the world has ever seen.

MAN IN CROWD I'm an Englishman . . . I'm the wrong colour . . .

HAMM The gentleman has drawn attention to the fact, the point I was making. We've got the same problems now as we had in the thirties, and they're now being made worse by the criminal lunacy of coloured immigration.

MAN IN CROWD I'm one of Mr Wilson's racialists – he made me a racialist – pudden-faced Wilson . . .

GENERAL VOICES Quite right, hear, hear . . .

MAN IN CROWD I'm an Englishman, and I'll speak my mind, but they won't put me on television. They'll put their drug takers and their long hair on television . . . I work twelve hours a day . . . and all the do-gooders . . . do-gooders on television, with their bloody long hair . . . I don't want to be on television. BBC ain't worth that . . .

But he was. And now he's in print too.

A Cause Worth Fighting For

Members of the British Battalion of the International Brigade

The Spanish Civil War – the first of the ideological wars of our time – began in 1936 when the Right-Wing Army, under one Colonel Francisco Franco, rebelled against the Republican Government in a struggle that lasted two-and-a-half years, with the world watching.

Before the Spanish War ended, leaving a million dead, it had cut a chasm through all Europe's loyalties and assumptions. It divided friend from friend, and brother from brother, and not only in Spain but in every country where the confrontation of right and left was coming to a head.

Not all the world was content to watch. Nazi Germany and Fascist Italy used Franco's war as a rehearsal of the greater war to come. Britain, however, was officially committed to non-intervention, as it was called.

Nevertheless hundreds of men and women took arms, as individuals, for what they judged to be the cause of freedom, and what others judged to be the cause of communism. They united in an irregular army of many nationalities and origins in what was called the International Brigade.

In years to come an illusion somehow grew that the Brigade was an army of radical romantics. Not so; the British volunteers were overwhelmingly workers. Britain in the Thirties was a sombre and uneasy place, taking its mood from the great Depression which had thrown three million on the dole. A bitter mood of disenchantment was only too ready to polarise into politics.

The British volunteers to the Brigade who remember it were not impartial witnesses to history. Was anyone impartial in the Spanish War?

One of them was a London furrier's assistant called Tony Gilbert.

TONY GILBERT I don't think anybody was ever recruited for the International Brigade, as far as I know. You volunteered; I volunteered after a meeting at the People's Palace – the speaker was Isabel Brown: a fantastic woman. She really made you feel that the men that were fighting Fascism in Spain were really fighting for the peace of the world.

Next morning I was working, for a change – one worked only three to four months in a year in those days, if one was lucky. I asked the boss for time off and went straight down to the International Brigade Office to volunteer.

The clandestine route from Paris to Spain was organised by one Josip Broz – who was later to have more public fame as Marshall Tito, President of Jugoslavia. He fixed their illegal passage over the frontier.

TONY GILBERT Then the bombs began to fall. There were no air raid shelters, and we were told to run for the open fields. Well, we turned round and laughed at each other. There were two volunteers, and there we were holding hands like two young kids, I suppose to help each other over our own feelings. We weren't really soldiers. We really didn't know what we were letting ourselves in for.

So this amateur army of miners and dockers and railwaymen and poets and political philosophers got down to learning how to be soldiers in a wholly foreign field.

TONY GILBERT The first time you hear a shell explode, the first time you hear it cut in the air, well it was for me a tremendously frightening experience. Your stomach just turns to water, and perhaps this happens to every soldier when he first hears the metal tearing through the air and knows he's liable to be finished.

Many were, too. Also, many deserted.

WILL PAYNTER I'm bound to say there were problems in the leadership of the British Battalion at the time which contributed to the desertions. Also personal problems – letters from home to the lads where the girlfriend was threatening to find some other friend, you know. Where the wife was desperate because of no money. So they deserted. Some got back to Britain and told their story to the press here. Others got arrested, and it was part of my job to get them from prison. In a war there is one penalty for a deserter, and it's usually pretty severe.

CLAUD COCKBURN Those people were always treated with the greatest sympathy and because of the institutions of political commissars in the Brigade, which meant to some extent political schoolmasters, every attempt was made to explain to those people how these things really worked, and to show them where theory and practice really intermesh.

Most of the British Press was committed in favour of the Franco side and against what they called the Reds. Stories of Communist atrocities were staple fare – the desecration of churches, the raping of nuns, and so on. And again, many of the stories were true. Churches were desecrated, images were destroyed. The fact was that by now the Government forces saw the identification of the Catholic Church with the Fascists as virtually complete.

However, even the most bitterly anti-clerical Spaniards were such ancestral Catholics that while they hated the Church they feared and respected the power of its symbols. Claud Cockburn remembers one specially powerful image that had to be physically executed.

CLAUD COCKBURN They didn't just think: well, all that nonsense. They continued to believe that this effigy had those magical powers, directed against them. So they tore down the effigy out of the church, and I think they fired two shots at it. But then somebody said: that's no good, just shooting at that thing. There ran through the village one of those little mountain single track railways. So they brought a kind of puffing billy which ran the railway, and they placed the effigy with its neck on the line, like people in those old films. And they got up steam, ran the train down the line and cut the head off the effigy. This, at last, had destroyed the evil power of this object.

Behind the men of the Brigade went the back-up units, the ambulance and medical teams. It was a tremendously difficult job.

MARGARET LESSER Of course, nurses and doctors were desperately needed. I was politically really Left-wing and I felt that this is the time when I must show that I will do something; I'll not only talk about it. I remember taking a last look with Walter de la Mare in mind when I crossed London Bridge. I only remember the first line now – Look your last on all things lovely.

It was a not a tidy war and it was not a tidy job. They were short of everything – doctors, nurses, plasma, drugs.

MARGARET LESSER Men poured in as fast as the few ambulances and trucks that we had could bring them in. I was the only nurse in the ward, and I had to decide who should be treated, and many died because I couldn't divide myself into six. And this was, of course, I think, the most terrible thing that happened to me in all my life.

The winter of 1937 was cruel. It was not what these people had expected of sunny Spain – this terrible Siberian snow of Aragon. In the battle of Teruel the British had a full company, 145 strong in the 15th Brigade, and the bitter cold and wretched clothes brought many casualties, not from Franco but from frostbite.

MARGARET LESSER We fairly frequently had to do amputations without anaesthetics. One man I can remember very well was brought in and said: 'You can take it off, if it has to come off, without anaesthetic. I can bear it'. And he did, and he didn't complain and nobody had to hold him down. The thing that seemed to grieve him most was that he wouldn't be able to fight anymore.

The International Brigade was of course never on the winning side. Their cause of Republican Spain had not just the Franco armies but a good deal of the world against them. They were forever on the retreat. Yet somehow morale remained.

BOB COONEY I can remember on hill 481 after a most terrible day – one company went through seven different company commanders, right down to a corporal who eventually became the commander of that company. But the Fascists knew we were still in good heart because we really made the air ring with our singing at night. You can't do this unless you have a certain basic morale already.

But the sands were running out for the Republicans, and even more so for the International Brigade. For Tony Gilbert the war was almost over.

TONY GILBERT We marched along this road. We heard this low hum, and then literally hundreds of tanks came from each side of the orange groves. I suppose in the first few minutes half of Number One company was killed, and the whole thing was impossible to continue. A hundred men were captured in that position. We believed we would be killed, and I think that except for a complete accident we would have been. I think if a carload of journalists hadn't arrived at the scene, American journalists they were, I don't believe we would have survived. They'd already pulled out machine guns. They'd already lined them up facing us and I do think we would have been quickly dealt with. But we weren't.

When Franco's men finally broke the line of the Ebro west of Catalonia, it really meant the end of the war. Just as Britain, ironically, was signing the deal with Munich, so were her citizens of the International Brigade coming to terms with defeat.

By the beginning of 1939 about 5000 men of 29 nationalities had passed through Barcelona on their way home, wherever that might be. In all, something like 13,000 foreigners fought for Republican Spain. Two thousand of them were British, of whom 500 were killed.

The surviving British volunteers were welcomed back to England by Major Attlee and Stafford Cripps. Before the last dismissal the Battalion had an English meal, which many of their poor shrunk stomachs could not accept. It was a day of sadness and bitterness.

MARGARET LESSER I didn't feel relief at being home. I felt bitter and angry; I didn't want to see or speak to anybody, except those I knew felt as I did. It shocked me that I felt like that.

TONY GILBERT I've got a British passport, but according to the letters I received when we got back from Spain, I'm not supposed to have a British passport until I repay them the amount of money they expended on my journey home, which I have never done. Incidentally, since then I've served five years in the British army fighting the same enemy. I really consider that they owe me a few years soldiers' wages, which isn't a great deal for the fighting I did against the same enemy, you know, before *they* entered the war.

And incidentally, there's not a single country in Eastern Europe where wounded International Brigaders aren't receiving pensions from their government. In fact, all International Brigaders in Socialist countries get pensions from their government. Not a single allowance from the British Government has ever been paid.

When I went to Spain I hated Fascism, and it seemed right for me to go and fight it, but I didn't understand the forces which were responsible for the development of Fascism. Philosophy was a word in a book for me. Understanding life, I think, began with my meeting men and women in Spain who really knew what it was about. I'm sure it's helped me to participate in facing the problem that confronts my class, the working class, and the British people in general.

Breaking the Silence

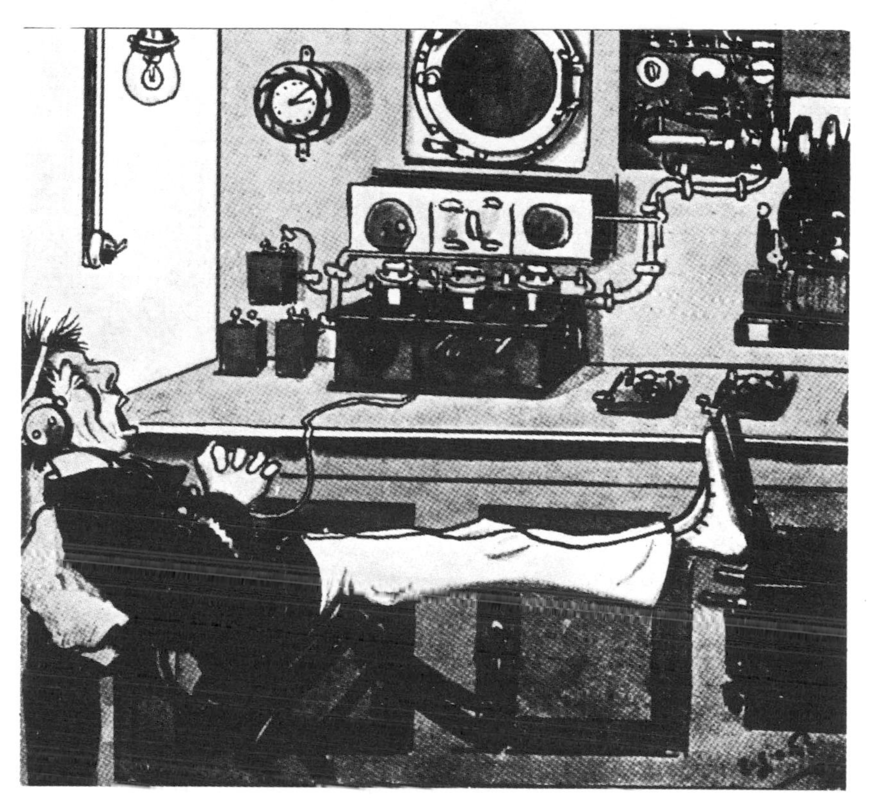

A cartoon from a 1913 Marconi Company publication

Everything that is now commonplace was once a miracle. Everything now taken for granted was, often remarkably recently, an unimagined mystery. Of course the things were always there. The cosmos existed before Galileo; gravity was in business before Newton. They had to await their historic moment to be revealed, defined, unbottled for the use of scientific man. The process has gone on since *homo,* on his way to becoming *sapiens,* discovered the first tool. It still goes on. It will go on forever, or until *homo sapiens* blunders on the last tool that will send him back to the protoplasm where it all began.

Radio, therefore, had been hanging around waiting to be discovered for thousands of years before Marconi. But it was as recently as 1896 that this Guglielmo Marconi, a talented electrical student from Leghorn and Pologna, came to London and developed his apparatus 'for the transmission of messages without the use of wires'. Six years later he succeeded in sending signals over the ocean. By 1907 there was a public wireless telegraph service over the Atlantic.

Young Marconi built better than he knew. By 1922 the air was full of noises; the first crude morse signals had turned into broadcasting as we know it now. But an awful lot of kitchen-table work had gone on before that. This young Italian Marconi formed his own British company, and R. D. Bangay joined it in 1903. He went to work at the experimental station at Glace Bay, Nova Scotia, to develop news transmissions to ships at sea, and then at Cape Cod in Massachusetts. One day a visitor turned up.

R.D. BANGAY It wasn't a local man, it was a man who came down from Boston, I think. He was a medical officer of some kind, and of course the station was surrounded by barbed wire fencing, and nobody was allowed in it. He came to the front door and asked whether he could have a look round and be shown the transmitters and things, and I asked him what his purpose was, and he calmly told me that he was writing a series . . . a thesis on the effect of electrical waves on the human brain. He said the electric waves softened the brain. So we fired him out of the transmitter house and everything else.

In 1906 the Russian Navy became interested. They ordered wireless apparatus to communicate with their ships, and Mr Bangay helped to install it. He completed a transmission, sent a signing-off message, and went back to the Russian base.

R. D. BANGAY And when I arrived there the first thing that happened was that I was arrested. I found later that I was arrested for having started a revolution, because some one of the officers had picked up my message saying I'd be ready the next morning at 9.30. That happened to be the very hour when the mutiny took place on one of their battleships, the Krasnigorka, and they thought that I had been mixed up in the revolution.

The Marconi-Wireless scenario got a splendid impetus through one of the great news stories of the period: the Crippen case. Dr Crippen, practising in North London, murdered his wife in 1910, and took off by transatlantic liner with his mistress Ethel Le Neve. They were actually intercepted on the way by the first police wireless message. This was dramatic enough to excite one John Scott Taggart.

SCOTT TAGGART I think the main thing that attracted me to wireless as a hobby way back in 1912 was the fact that you could communicate, it was a real working hobby. You were doing what commercial people were doing, you were doing what ships were doing. You were doing what Marconi was doing.

In 1913 a British ship called the *Volturno* laden with Jewish refugees from east Europe caught fire in mid-Atlantic. She had wireless, and sent out an SOS. John Scott Taggart was listening in.

SCOTT TAGGART 160 people lost their lives, but 600 were saved, and that was done entirely by wireless. The last message the operator sent was 'For God's sake can't anybody come and help us'. Well, ten ships went to help them, and I got all the messages in connection with the Volturno. I knew all the names of the people who were rescued, and survivors' own stories that were sent by wireless to the British newspapers and so on. It was a tremendous boost for ships' wireless communication. And of course it was very exciting for a boy of sixteen.

This 'wireless' was now a matter of public interest, especially in hobby-papers and boys' books. One of these pieces hooked Eric Payne, also destined for the Marconi Company.

PAYNE My first contact came with an article in the Book of Knowledge, a very high class monthly publication, subscribed to by all the best families. It was edited by Arthur Mee. In June of 1911, there appeared an article entitled 'The Unseen Telegraph Messenger', and it described in considerable detail a wireless transmitter and receiver in those days. Another zealot was my neighbour, the vicar of Stoke-by-Nayland.

Canon Wilkinson first used the Church tower to support his aerial, but I think the parishioners took rather a poor view of this, so in his own garden in the vicarage he constructed a very wonderful mast, quite a hundred feet high. He was meticulous about the joints. He contended that the joints should be soldered. He called it sodder because in the days of King Solomon's temple the Bible refers to the sodderers who had helped to make the metal for the temple. And Canon Wilkinson insisted on soddering these joints up at the top, so he got himself hauled up the mast by his family with the blow lamp heating the soldering iron in a bath tub. He hauled this right up to the top and he did his joins. And he admitted afterwards that he was crying with fear because of the height and the risks.

The wireless had of course now become an international obsession. The country was full of enthusiastic amateurs eaves-dropping on everything that came their way. One of them, Kenneth Alford, was tuned in to the German transmission from Nauern, outside Berlin.

KENNETH ALFORD I noticed that he was sending out one particular sentence time after time: *Krieg ist erklaart gegen Russland und Frankreich* – War is declared against France and Russia. This is probably the most exciting message I have ever taken. And we go to the log and we see: August 2nd, 1914, European War broke out, a series of calls received and the blank space showing that the post office had impounded the whole equipment. That closes the book.

The new development was the radio-valve, which made possible the transmission of speech. One of the first people ever to talk over the air was Mrs Donisthorpe, the wife of an Army officer.

MRS DONISTHORPE We had groups of training centres all round Worcester. He had a tent on the river bank where he had his special experiments, his own, nothing to do with the Army except that he used Army stuff and Army personnel. During the night I used to have to go down there and play gramophone records and talk to my husband over the radio, and I used to say, I remembered that rhyme: A wonderful bird the pelican, his beak can hold more than his belly can. I used to say that endlessly on the radio, I don't know why, I don't know whether the vowels sounds and the consonants were any help.

Mrs Donisthorpe later heard that a German Zeppelin on a night cruise picked up her message. It puzzled them greatly. They went to great lengths to de-code it, and eventually shrugged it off as one more incomprehensible English eccentricity.

There was of course no 'broadcasting' as we know it today. But sometime in the 20s a little Dutch station, PCGG, used to come up for wireless amateurs, and our sets over here could pick up those Dutch Concerts, as they were called. Then the British wireless amateurs organised themselves into a lobby, a pressure-group strong enough to oblige the Government to let Marconis initiate experimental broadcasts from Writtle, near Chelmsford. A very early broadcaster was from a local amateur concert-party: Winifred Sayer.

WINIFRED SAYER We were in more or less a packing shed, there were big wooden cases and that all around. We sort of had to walk and step over them and all the equipment to find where Mr Ditcham was sitting with – I don't know what you call it, all the valves and things. He had a table and talked at a microphone.

There was a song at that time that was quite popular, it was very short, it was called Absent. Don't ask me who wrote it because I couldn't tell you. But I sang that. But of course we didn't have a piano, we had to start off with a tuning fork. The electrical things were going on at the same time. I think I got ten shillings a night. I thought it was wealth. It's a long time you know.

As a matter of fact it was not very long ago. Broadcasting began in the lifetime of many people still in it. Finally the Government allowed five big wireless manufacturers to combine into the British Broadcasting Company, with the call sign: 2 LO. This ultimately became the British Broadcasting Corporation, with the results you hear and see before you now, for good or ill.

The Tithe War

East Anglia poster protesting against tithes

The British people, of all kinds, have always been given to complaining about authority – often with plenty of reason. Sometimes when the complaining got nowhere they have been driven to doing something about it – what has now come to be called 'direct action', or physical protest. It gave birth to the phrase 'standing up to be counted' – a good phrase, if you meant it, like breaking the law if the cause was just. There is a long tradition of it, from the Tolpuddle Martyrs, from the Luddites and the Glasgow Cotton Spinners in the last century, down to the suffragettes and the CND in ours. Sometimes it has worked and sometimes it hasn't.

Some of the protesters were protecting their consciences, some were protecting their lives, some were just the English bourgeois eccentrics exercising their idiosyncratic right to snub the Establishment. That last – the middle-class revolt – was rare enough, but once it came to pass.

The great Depression of the 20s and early 30s hit everyone, in the towns and on the land. Farmers in East Anglia do well today; they did badly then. There was little they could do about it, but one thing they could do was refuse to pay their Tithes.

This was an extraordinary levy imposed on farmers by, of all institutions, the Church of England. Originally it had been a simple tithe, a tenth, of the farmers' produce, sequestered to keep up the local Church. It was now levied in simple cash, a kind of freelance taxation, again just to sustain the Church. Many hard-up farmers did not see the sense, let alone the justice, of this. So they demonstrated, in a rather unexpected way. Their leader in Suffolk was A. G. Mobbs.

A. G. MOBBS Well, we more or less took up the position of passive resistance. It wasn't a question of breaking the law, we simply allowed the law to take its course, and put up with the consequences.

This Mr Mobbs, a gardener and a dairy farmer, was not the sort of man you would expect to meet at the barricades – nor were any of the other fighters in the tithe war. There was the Prime Minister's niece, Lady Eve Balfour. There was Doreen Rash, who was better known as the novelist Doreen Wallace, and her farmer husband; and a Quaker artist and smallholder Philip Butler.

In East Anglia it became a sort of holy war between the farmers and the Church. It was a sort of ritual that went on for years. But it came down to this. The farmers wouldn't pay their tithes. So the bailiffs were sent in to sequester goods and animals in lieu. But the farmers saw to it that the removal was going to be made very, very difficult.

In May 1932 there was a farm near Ipswich belonging to a Mr Westren. The bailiffs had moved in and seized six corn-stacks, in lieu of tithe. They had been successfully tendered for by the Ecclesiastical Commissioners.

One morning the armada was sighted on the horizon: a fleet of lorries headed for the farm. Villagers rang the church bells to call up help. One of the first to arrive was Philip Butler, the Quaker.

PHILIP BUTLER One of the lorries came up the drive and began to load corn-stacks. The locals got hold of an old wagon, pulled it along and put it across the drive. They dug a trench across the gateway, to make it difficult for the lorry to go back again onto the main road.

A. G. MOBBS And somebody had a brilliant idea – I don't know who, it may have even been Mr Westren himself. Anyhow, he set his men to fell a very big tree that would have fallen over the roadway to the entrance to the stackyard, and the lorries would have never got away that night. Anyhow, these fellows with the lorries were so worried and upset about it that they went on strike and refused to pitch any more sheafs.

PHILIP BUTLER Well, I can tell you, there was a very great cheer went up from the crowd standing all around. And, of course, we had to celebrate a little bit. Mr Westren's workmen were very interested – it was a serious thing for them, because if those stacks had been taken, one of the mainstays of the farm would have gone, and some of their wages. So we held a meeting in the stackyard – had a wagon, stood upon it, and delivered ourselves – Mr Mobbs and myself – about the whole question of tithe. We had a very big audience. Everybody went off in a very good humour.

The early thirties were the great days of the tithe war. The Church was determined to get its money, and there was a somewhat shady company called General Dealers Limited that seemed to be working for the Ecclesiastical Commissioners to do the tendering and carting away the stuff.

The farmers got up to all manner of tricks to make it awkward – and of course to get publicity for their cause, which was the whole idea.

One of them who organised a dramatic defence at her farm was Lady Eve Balfour.

LADY EVE Well, we had locked the gate and we left unlocked a little gate beside it . . . a footpath gate. If they had done the correct thing – which would have been to come in on the unlocked gate and come up to the house: ask for me, present a warrant, I should have gone down with a key, and I would have opened the big gate. We chained the big gate and we fastened to it a string which led to a shotgun with a blank cartridge in it.

A. G. MOBBS When the police arrived they opened the gate, and off went the gun. One of the police said: 'Good God, this place is mined!'

Lady Eve Balfour lost her cattle, but she made the headlines, and that was the whole idea. Publicity was the object, the more the better.

It is interesting to speculate what a contemporary current-affairs television programme would have done with all this. They would have made a meal of it. The cameras would certainly have been down to Wortham Manor, near Diss, where Rowland Rash and his wife, the novelist Doreen Wallace, owed several hundred pounds in unpaid tithes, and were as determined as everyone else to be as obstructive and bloody-minded as possible within the law. Early one morning the invaders turned up in a fleet of lorries to seize £700 worth of pigs and cattle.

DOREEN RASH They came up the hill from the church, all in a row. The names on them indicated that they came from the North of England, where, of course, tithe is almost unknown. So they could cart their pigs without feeling a bad conscience to themselves, you see. They didn't know what they were up against, these lorrymen.

The trench that we had dug, was really dug at the behest of the road authorities – who wanted a nice drainage for the road which had been flooding. They didn't tell us to dig it quite so deep, quite so wide as we eventually did. Anything you can do on your own ground, except, I suppose, where you must leave access for distrained stock.

ROWLAND RASH The place had a barrier across the front of the building: a steam engine, a threshing drum, and an elevator – so it was impossible to get a lorry in for loading the pigs.

DOREEN RASH It was a very effectual barrier. That's why they had these separate – one pig – little sedan-chair affairs: to lift them. And it took a very long time.

When they were heaving these pigs on to the lorries they used a method which is not allowed in British markets: the 'ear and tail' method. Pick up piggy by his tail and one ear and he screams blue murder. So one of us mentioned it to the policeman and said, 'You must stop that, you know, you don't allow it on market.' Which was all to the good, you know, it all made our bit of publicity in the papers.

In this case it paid off. For a County Court judge had witnessed this battle of the pigs, and A. G. Mobbs was present at an important sequel.

A. G. MOBBS I was at the Chamber of Commerce Dinner when the then Minister of Agriculture, a Mr Walter Elliot, was the principal speaker. Judge Herbert Smith – the judge in question – was one of the after-dinner speakers. To my utter amazement, he set about the Minister for all he was worth. He told him – he said: 'Look, I have perfectly honourable, straightforward men coming to my court with what appears to be a just grievance.' And he said 'You've got to do something about it. It's up to the Government to enquire into the whole thing and set up a Committee of Enquiry or a Royal Commission.'

And within a month the Government decided to set up a Royal Commission, which sat for 18 months: and to which I myself gave evidence.

So did Lady Eve Balfour, and all the rest of them. The Royal Commission's recommendation was a small reduction in the tithe payments, and an end to the whole thing in 1996. The Tithe Payers' Association, which wanted and had fought for abolition, thought this was preposterous. In June 1936 they had a great demonstration in London. Five thousand farmers from Suffolk and Norfolk marched through the City of London to Westminster.

DOREEN RASH The march on London was one of our best publicity stunts. They came from wherever we had a Tithe Payers Branch . . . Londoners just flocked, because this was something absolutely new, something they had never seen before.

PHILIP BUTLER I stopped to speak to some of them. I said, 'Well, what do you think of this?' 'Oh, we are glad to see you here, it's time you came.' They were all on our side. It had got so far that even the people in London understood what it was all about.

None of all this made any real difference; the Bill became law. The Government took over the collection of tithes, and paid the Church £70 million compensation. They reduced the tithe by a miserable 20%, and said it would stop after 60 years; by then the £70 million would be redeemed. It was a slight victory, which was only marginally better than nothing.

But – forty years later, in 1976, the victory became practically total. Parliament was told that as from October 1977 the collection of tithes would be suspended – simply because collecting them would become too expensive. So that was the end of the tithe war – no more tithes. And that was that.

The Great Scuttle

Scapa Flow after the scuttling of the German fleet

A couple of hours sailing northward from Scotland lie the Islands of Orkney, dividing the North Sea from the Atlantic and enclosing within them the traditional anchorage of the British Fleet – Scapa Flow.

Today the mailboat which makes the passage between the mainland and the islands sails through almost deserted waters. Yet on one day, more than half a century ago, one of the most extraordinary episodes in the history of the sea took place in Scapa Flow. It begins on Armistice Day 1918 and ends on Midsummer Day 1919.

The Armistice of November 1918 emptied Scapa Flow of its warships. In practical terms the War was over, but an Armistice is not a Peace; it was only a cease-fire to allow a permanent situation to be negotiated. One of its terms was that the German High Seas Fleet should be interned in a neutral port, pending a Peace Treaty. In fact, the German Fleet was obliged to anchor – with doubtful legality – in the heart of the enemy's sovereignty, in the wartime base of the British Grand Fleet, Scapa Flow.

In November 1918 Captain R.C.V. Ross, R.N., was young enough to think of the war as an adventure that was coming to an untimely end.

ROSS I was only a midshipman, about 17½, and quite frankly the Armistice came to us as a bit of an anticlimax. It wasn't like people on the Western Front who suddenly knew they weren't going to be killed, you know. To us, it was – well it was the end of our chance of having another go at the German Fleet. I think the Armistice really came as a disappointment.

In the Kaiser's Navy the mood was heavy with defeat. At the time Vizeadmiral Friedrich Ruge was a sub-lieutenant on a German destroyer.

RUGE After we knew the Armistice conditions, my flotilla – I think it was the 21st of November, at 8 o'clock – we had to be 50 miles east of the Firth of Forth. That was all we knew. I was in what we called a *grosses Torpedoboot,* they now call them destroyers, very fast, 36 knots, very good boats, 105-millimetre guns. I was gunnery officer.

ROSS I was in HMS *Malaya* in the Fifth Battle Squadron at Rossyth, and we were told that the Germans were going to come in past May Island into the Forth. The whole British Fleet went out, headed by Sir David Beatty, of course, in the flagship the *Queen Elizabeth,* in two lines. The Germans were to steam slowly up in between these lines.

In the British ships there was tension; they were sailing to meet a fleet they had met only once before, at the Battle of Jutland. No one wholly believed that the great German ships would come harmlessly within range. Aboard was ex-Leading Seaman W.G. Waterson, who had joined the navy at fifteen and a half, only four months before the ending of the war.

WATERSON We closed up at action stations. We was all ready for opening up if they'd opened up on us, you see. We had the cartridges up from the – from the magazine, and *everyone* was action stations.

Here then was the once great Imperial German Fleet which, since Jutland, had never left its home ports to fight again. The morale of its men had degenerated, even collapsed into mutiny and revolt. Now it emerged at half steam, disarmed, to make the bitter journey to captivity. A great array of 74 vessels – 5 battle cruisers, 11 battleships, 8 light cruisers, 50 destroyer torpedo boats: the great names of the High Seas Fleet: Hindenburg, Friedrich der Grosse, Seydlitz, Kaiser, Derfflinger, Bayern, Kron-Prinz Wilhelm, ships for which the British Navy had waited and watched for two and a half years in vain.

ROSS The curious thing was that when we actually saw these German ships for the first time, we saw them just as we'd always studied them as recognition silhouettes. You could say to yourself, that's a Konigsclass battleship, or that's a Kaiserclass battleship with its funnels slightly further apart, just as you'd learnt it.

And then Admiral Beatty suddenly gave the Germans their orders: their destination was not a neutral port at all, but Scapa Flow.

Most of the crews were repatriated to a Germany prostrate in ruin and defeat. Only skeleton crews were left to take the ships into internment, under their Admiral von Reuter.

Today the little town of Stromness at the mouth of the Flow looks much as it did in 1918. The people of Orkney have watched ships come and go since the Vikings, but the Fleet which sailed into the anchorage that November must surely have been the strangest of all. One of the young schoolgirls who saw it arrive was Mrs Rosetta Groundwater. She and her sister went with their father to a vantage point over the Flow.

MRS GROUNDWATER With a pair of binoculars we saw rather dejected looking vessels entering the Flow. They looked quite different from the British Navy; they were tidy and trim and the Germans were all rusty and probably discoloured with the camouflage paint.

It was a dark day; it was in the late afternoon, as far as I can remember, and the light wasn't very good, but we could make out what was happening. I think we were there about an hour, and we saw a good many of them. I think the Hindenburg was the biggest one of all.

The big ships dropped anchor. The destroyers were tied to mooring buoys in pairs. The British pilot gave Lieutenant Ruge a warning about the Scapa weather.

RUGE What impressed me was the deep respect your officer had for the winter gales in Scapa Flow. He told us to secure the boats very thoroughly; and first we did it in our usual way with steel ropes only. He said, no, that would *not* be sufficient and then we took a length of chain out of the chain locker and put it round. And then in the winter it was just sufficient. We sent home most of the crews.

Out of 130-140 men on one of our destroyers, only 20 stayed, and that was how I was made a commanding officer. I was a very junior officer, I could never have been commanding a destroyer like that. And then the British came and took away all our boats with the exception of one whaler per destroyer; we were strictly forbidden to go ashore.

This harsh rule, which deprived the German sailors of any recreation or exercise on the islands which lay so near, was enforced by the First Battle Squadron of the Royal Navy on duty in the Flow.

ROSS There were about five battleships in the Flow looking after the German Fleet and a sprinkling of destroyers; we simply had orders to see that they didn't raise steam to break out of the Flow. Not that they wanted to, and I doubt if they could have, but those were the orders, and also that they didn't attempt a landing party.

RUGE The winter was the worst time because the days were very short. In spring, we could sometimes sit on deck, and we found we could play tag. Playing tag around funnels of destroyers – quite an experience.

The German crews were a constant object of curiosity to the British seamen on the guard ships.

WATERSON A chap had a set of – what do you call them? Parallel bars, he was doing gymnastics. And then of course the old occupation, walking up and down the fo'c'sle, same as British sailors do. You used to see them there fishing over the side. Of course we did, you know, too.

RUGE In spring the fish suddenly left us completely and there we were without any fresh meat. And then we saw the seagulls flying about and said to ourselves, we tried to shoot them, but the only weapon we had was a signal pistol. We never did get one.

ROSS We sat there doing our normal routine. In a ship life goes on just the same even if there are 20 or 30 German ships a mile away. But the patrols went round looking at them, occasionally went alongside and said 'you're making too much smoke, are you lighting up the second boiler?' and they would say, 'Oh, no we're only flashing up or doing our laundry.' They'd look rather sad.

While we were talking to them on deck our sailors down below were probably swopping a bar of soap for an iron cross or something like that you see, through the port holes.

RUGE We liked to sing these folk songs and I had a guitar. We'd assemble on deck and sing together. And we had a gramophone but the regulator broke, and from that time we used it mostly for waking up the people there sleeping in the rooms around our common wardroom.

So the months dragged by. May brought the anniversary of that fierce but inconclusive naval battle that the British call Jutland, but which the Germans call Skaggerak.

RUGE We said, why don't we show them what we think about Jutland? Our admiral had sent round an order not to do anything, which was sensible, but it had not reached us because mail arrangements were somewhat hazy up there. We kind of dressed ship, but we were not allowed to do so between the masts and funnels. It was quite effective.

There was some commotion on the British guard destroyer and the boat came over, two officers, and one asked me in German: 'What's the meaning of those flags?' First I said in the German expression: 'Skaggerak' and they didn't understand. Then I said 'Battle of Jutland', and they just turned and went back. In the meantime we got orders from our Admiral to stop that nonsense. So we stopped it.

Von Reuter, Admiral of the interned fleet, had been kept in ignorance by the British of the progress of the peace negotiations. But on 20 June he read in a week-old copy of *The Times* newspaper, that the peace terms had to be accepted or rejected by the next day. What no one had bothered to tell him was that the Armistice had been extended by a further 48 hours.

All the Admiral surmised, however, was that by noon on 21 June, next day, the treaty had to be signed or there would be a state of war again. In which case, von Reuter argued, the British would take their ships by force. He decided to send orders to prepare to scuttle the Grand Fleet.

Soon after sunrise on that 21 June another baffling thing happened: the British guard squadron weighed anchor and sailed out of the Flow. The Germans watched with consternation. They were persuaded that the Armistice would expire in a few hours. The British squadron had never left Scapa Flow for months. At once the Germans assumed that the Squadron was about to join the Major Fleet and come in through the various entrances and take them.

In reality the move had no sinister purpose at all. The British had simply gone out on a torpedo exercise. But it confirmed the German command in its decision: they would sink their Fleet.

That same morning in Stromness, Rosetta Groundwater's school was preparing a treat.

MRS GROUNDWATER On Midsummer Day in 1919, the school was promised a trip to see the German Fleet, and we went down on the water boat, the Flying Kestrel. It used to carry water from Stromness to the fleet. A lovely morning, the sea was beautifully calm, and we sailed down right through the ships quite slowly.

They were all rusty and dirty. The men were dirty too. And idle, that was the bit that struck me, that there was no bustle going on at all; it was just sort of utter dejection. Made us quite sad seeing them.

RUGE First we saw the Flying Kestrel, the steamer from Kirkwall, I think it is – with at least 300 schoolchildren on board. And then we saw people running aboard on the upper deck of the battle cruiser Siedlitz. That had never happened at Scapa Flow before in seven months, because there was no need to run at any time. And then we saw the signal coming slowly through the line. Our commanding officer, Captain Lieutenant Mansche, gave the order to scuttle our boats.

And now we went to our stations. I had prepared a lot, because I didn't trust the sea valves, because so much things had grown at the bottom of our ships. I didn't think they would work.

I had a very strong stoker, I think he was a prize boxer or something. We had prepared certain tubes and pipes with sea water in the boiler rooms and had let big hammers alongside, and he went down from one room to the other and destroyed these pipes.

Some of them, young stokers, started packing up their things. It was a funny feeling to hear the water rushing in everywhere, and those quietly, calmly packing their things and taking their time about it. I speeded them up a bit. Then we went aft and went into the boats. We had only four whalers for 56 people. And my B.112 was rather deep down in the water already.

MRS GROUNDWATER The first I noticed was one ship that seemed to be very low in the water, and the men coming off into small boats. And waving a dirty white flag. And then another ship almost right beside us turned right over, and water and steam shot up through the empty stopcocks. And then another ship went down in a swirl of water, and we were ordered to stop.

A British destroyer started steaming up and the Germans were in boats. While we were waiting to know what to do we saw a British officer shoot a German. He wouldn't put up his hands to surrender and they shot him, and he just dropped right in the water. You know, we'd never seen pictures or anything, and it seemed to us as if they were enacting a story for our benefit. We didn't realise what was happening. Nobody told us.

RUGE I took the helm. Fortunately we had a following wind in the direction of the island of Fara, 500 yards away perhaps. We approached it very, very slowly. Then one of the drifters came up firing wildly.

Before they could do any harm to us, they saw our senior officer of destroyers going down into a boat. He had put on his best uniform with three stripes. They swore at him and tried to stop him, but he simply waved them away. And then they were quiet and we got to the island of Fara unmolested.

I saw my own boat going down first. I was rather relieved. And the sun shone and the stones were quite warm and we took our seats to see all the ships going down.

Meanwhile, on the torpedo-exercise, Boy Seaman Waterson was on duty in Royal Sovereign.

WATERSON At that time I was a boy signals office messenger, just underneath the signal platform. I hadn't been on watch long, the afternoon watch. The chief yeoman came in and I could see he was in a bit of a tizz, as we used to say. He had a signal in his hand and he said, get this round as fast as your legs can carry you, laddie.

Away I nipped through the bulkhead door. I thought it must be important for him to bring it down. So of course I had a look at it, and it was from HMS Westcott, the guard destroyer: 'The German Fleet sinking'. I thought well, good God. They haven't been sunk with gunfire, they haven't been torpedoed, they must have turned the sea cocks on and scuttled them.

ROSS We were in the middle of picking up our torpedoes after this exercise, when suddenly a signal arrived. First signal said 'The German Fleet appears to be sinking' and within a few minutes a second signal came 'German Fleet *are* sinking at their moorings'.

Well, we went as fast as we could and in through the Pentland Firth, in past Swona and Switha and in through Hoxa Gate into the Flow, and there we really saw the *most* extraordinary sight I've ever seen in my life.

Here were these huge battleships and battle cruisers in every sort of stage of sinking. Some were going down in a sort of orderly way, you know, their funnels and masts still sticking out when they got to the bottom. Others were rolling over, and some were kind of plunging down doing a 'Titanic'. Some of the ships as they plunged under made a horrible sort of rumbling noise – I've only heard of it in accounts of the Titanic sinking, but when a ship takes a final dive all the stuff inside that's loose casts adrift and rolls about and you get this sort of death rattle of a ship.

The Captain picked out one ship that hadn't sunk very far, a cruiser called the Frankfurt, and he sent the First Lieutenant and me and some sailors over and we went on board. There weren't many Germans about but there was one Petty Officer and we got hold of him and I told him in my school German that he'd got to stop the ship sinking and he told me back that he couldn't – which was perfectly true – they'd done this very efficiently. There are a lot of holes in a ship's hull and every single one was open and all the wheels for shutting them again had been taken off and thrown overboard and the shafts had been sawn through. So their sea-cocks were open, their condenser inlets, their torpedo tubes, and they were flooding quickly.

RUGE On the island of Fara we had a picnic, we opened a tin of bully beef and ate that. Because it was one of my men said, scuttle makes hungry.

Then we were told to go into our boats again and we were towed to the British Battle Squadron. When we came into the open we saw that the Hindenburg was still afloat surrounded by British tugs and guard boats, and one of my men said, 'She should go down, she should go down'. The Hindenburg suddenly righted itself, went down. But it was not very deep there and the upper turrets, masts and funnels still showed, but she had gone down.

MRS GROUNDWATER We saw the Hindenburg slowly sinking, her decks awash. I think it was the Siedlitz that turned right over, and there was one that went down and was just the part of it sticking up at a curious angle. The others were being rushed ashore to beach them on the islands.

RUGE Our party went aboard the Royal Oak. The first impression was going up that immense ladder and quarterdeck. I had not been in big ships like the Royal Oak since 1915. Very impressive. And then this large and splendidly white quarterdeck, and a lot of our officers and men there. I had always kept my guitar with me. One British officer came to me and said, keep off the paintwork; I had leaned my guitar to British paint, and so he kicked it away.

Then we got orders to appear on the middle deck, and there the captain of the Royal Oak assembled the Officers only, and read a paper to them, beginning: 'By this act of treachery we had forfeited being treated as real sailors' and things like that, you know.

We didn't like it very much, and our captain was the man who spoke the best English, because he was half-Scottish, and he at once went up to him and told him at once we didn't accept it. And the captain of the Royal Oak simply grinned a tiny bit and said 'I've orders to read it'. And that was that; we knew his opinion about it.

MRS GROUNDWATER When we came back to Stromness the pier was just crowded. I think every parent must have been there. We couldn't understand why they looked so anxious; we had enjoyed the whole thing so much. And then they told us we'd been in among the sinking of the German Fleet and we'd been in great danger with all this action going on so close to us; for we were only a small ship compared to some of these big ones. So it was only then that it struck us that we'd seen something that was really of historical importance.

ROSS Our feeling at the time was really – as junior officers you know – not the Admiralty's feeling, or the Government's, that we'd been cheated. These ships had been sent there to be surrendered, as we thought, and we thought it was rather a dirty trick to scuttle yourself like that. But that was by no means the official view, and nor was it the Germans' view, of course. The Germans thought they were saving their honour – and I've no reason to quarrel with that view from their point of view.

RUGE We were kind of fatalistic at that time. It was sad, but the general feeling was of relief. It seemed the best solution to us at that time. We were quite proud of it, I must say.

The Jarrow Crusade

The Jarrow marchers lining up for food at Lavendon, near Bedford

In the 7th Century a North Country monk called the Venerable Bede wrote the first history of England, and indeed invented the word 'Englishman'. His monastery was in a place virtually unknown, called Jarrow. Thirteen hundred years later the name came to mean a great deal more.

The 1930s were a period known – rather ruefully now – as the Depression. About two million in this small island were out of work. Nowhere were things worse than in Jarrow, in County Durham. Jarrow made ships – or had done so once – and virtually nothing else, from the iron ore to the rolling mills to the graving yard. And the greatest of the yards was Palmers, on the south bank of the Tyne. Palmers was Jarrow, they used to say, and Jarrow was Palmers. They were totally mutually dependent.

In 1931 the cruiser 'York' was launched. That was the very last ship. No more orders. Palmers closed. Three-quarters of Jarrow went on the dole.

Worse still: Palmers was sold to National Shipbuilding Securities, a consortium of shipowners whose proviso was that the yard could build no more ships for 40 years. That, for a ship-building craftsman, now meant a lifetime on the dole.

Jarrow's MP was a fiery and ardent little red-headed Socialist called Ellen Wilkinson. She called Jarrow 'the murdered town'. There was also a young reporter called Ritchie Calder, who became Lord Ritchie-Calder, who knew the region well.

RITCHIE CALDER In Jarrow you saw the face of hunger in the nineteen thirties. You weren't seeing it on a poster; you weren't seeing it on the telly; you were seeing hunger in your own street, in your own mirror.

Paddy Scullion was a young Councillor of this hopeless town.

PADDY SCULLION In them times people, many people would think that to go on a march was all wrong. We had a very religious body in the town who believed that unemployment was a cross to bear. That was the mentality of some people.

JOAN CLARK Week by week you could see them all getting a little more morose trying to keep cheerful, stopping out all day. They knew it was hopeless before they went out looking for a job – take a walk, take the ferry over to Howden. A walk to Newcastle was nothing to most of them.

Deputations to the Board of Trade in London met with icy indifference by Walter Runciman. Let Jarrow, he said, work out its own salvation.

Very well, said Joe Symonds, one of Palmers unemployed and later an MP, let us try.

JOE SYMONDS We decided; why not a march to London? We can show them that with all our adversity that we have still a bit of spirit left.

Councillor David Riley was chosen to be Marshall of the march.

DAVID RILEY It was first intended that we should call it the Jarrow Hunger March. When I was made the Marshall of the march, I said that was not a very nice name; I said Crusade would be a better title.

RITCHIE CALDER This was a proper march, I mean proper in the British constitutional sense. The town council of Jarrow met in solemn session and all parties decided on the march, and this was approved by the mayor and the corporation and all duly minuted and official.

DAVID RILEY We had to think about the accommodation we could get. The most convenient figure we could arrive at was 200. We had a number of Halls in the town, where anybody could put their name down to go to the March. We'd have a clerk there, and a doctor to come along and examine everybody to see if they were fit to do a march job.

JOAN CLARK I don't think people ever realise: we did three months preparation to that march before the men moved off from the Town Hall steps.

From Jarrow in the North East to London in the South is some 300 miles. It was agreed to limit each day's march to 10 to 20 miles. The marchers were under very strict orders. Anyone who misbehaved would be sent home at once. There was to be no begging, no roadside collecting. The organisation and the logistics were formidable – the assembling of beds and blankets and cooking gear.

DAVID RILEY We were at our wits end to know how we were going to do all this. And the Northern Bus people said: Well listen, I tell you what, we'll sell you a bus for £100. If you bring it back to us, we'll buy it back for £100.

SAM ROWAN The money started to roll in, and the Borough Treasurer was receiving the funds and issuing official receipts. Then it was suddenly realised that this money had to be properly accounted for, and the Treasurer was then in quite a fix. You know how volunteers are picked, of course, so they picked me.

Ellen Wilkinson took charge of the Petition which she was to lay at the bar of the House of Commons. It had more than 12,000 signatures.

The departure was the biggest turnout Jarrow had ever known. The march set off in good heart, led by the Mayor and the Council. The political parties abandoned their differences in support for the Crusade; the Labour and the Tory agents both joined in. During the whole of this march of 200 workless men there was no disorganisation, not one single complaint from the police. The marchers cleaned up scrupulously behind them. They were welcomed all along the line.

RITCHIE CALDER The morale of the march was remarkable because they had something to do, for the first time. They'd get up, just knowing they had a purpose. They hadn't had a purpose for five, ten, fifteen years.

We slept on hard boards. We carried our packs with us, our groundsheets and so on, and slept hard. It was good for me, a good training for the Aldermaston march thirty years later.

Right in the middle of the march a curious thing happened, which dates the occasion exactly. It seems that suddenly the great scandal of the 30s surfaced: the story of King Edward VIII and Mrs Simpson. It had been fairly common knowledge in America for weeks, but it had been effectively smothered in Britain. Ritchie Calder, who was on the *Daily Herald* then, and Ellen Wilkinson had some hints of what was going on.

RITCHIE CALDER Ellen and I were walking along in the column and we were talking about the King and Mrs Simpson.

And came the midday break and we saw the people going around talking, groups were breaking up and then finally a deputation came to Ellen and to me, and said: What's it all about, the King and that woman? We tried to pass it off rather lightly, and they were absolutely furious with us, for repeating the story. Then when they began to realise that in fact it was true they were furious with him. The King believed he had the people of the country behind him. He didn't understand that the people of Jarrow had nothing, except the family. This symbolically became the threat to the family, and they were very angry.

Then, while the march was crossing Yorkshire, the Government in London suddenly and for no special reason suddenly announced that the Crusade would not be received at Downing Street.

RITCHIE CALDER The Government had completely lost the meaning of this march. We weren't marching to the Government; we weren't marching to Number Ten Downing Street. We were marching to Parliament, with a perfectly constitutional right to present the Petition to Parliament. We carried it all the way, with all these signatures.

By the time the marchers reached the half-way mark the hard, hard road was beginning to have its effect.

DAVID RILEY The men's boots were beginning to wear and the Marshall of the march went out and saw the trade unions. They said if we sent the men's boots in they would be returned the following morning. We never paid them, but whether the firm gave them extra money for it or not I don't know. But next morning everybody got their right shoes back again, and they were all very glad of it.

The Jarrow Crusade approached London in atrocious weather and good spirits. They had had, for the first time for years, in some cases – fresh air, exercise, regular meals. Throughout the length of England they had met with goodwill and hospitality from their fellow-men that they did not realise any longer existed. Capitalists in Harrogate, Leeds and Sheffield had dined them with decency, Co-Ops and Trades Unions had mended their boots and replaced their clothes. They entered London on 21 October, after 27 long days on the road.

In the last stages Communists and Fascists equally tried to infiltrate the column, but the Jarrow men, being Jarrow men, closed their ranks: this was their Crusade.

On 3 November Edward VIII, whose Mrs Simpson affair had caused such a fuss on the way, opened Parliament. The Jarrow men were given a place on The Mall to see him pass. The next day the new House would be presented with their Petition.

In it, the citizens of Jarrow 'humbly and anxiously prayed that His Majesty's Government would realise the urgent need that work be provided for the town, that they might be relieved of their present distress and misery and might look forward to the future with trust and dignity.'

This was, alas, a bad time to ask for Parliament's consideration. Within weeks the Constitution they so hopefully invoked was overwhelmed by the melodrama of the Abdication. A world war was round the corner. And in the end, of course, it was Adolf Hitler's Germany, not Baldwin's Britain, that solved the problems of Jarrow.

JOE SYMONDS You had to see this march in complete detail to understand why it was different. The bearing of the men made it different, the method they adopted was different. That made it stand out.

PADDY SCULLION The difference between them marches and today's marches was the fact that we had something to fight for, something real, the right not for increased unemployment benefits or increased money, but for the right to work, which belongs to all men.

The Narrow Boat Men

Chocolate Charlie Atkins

Not all that long ago the inland waterways of England were the commercial highways of the land, two thousand miles of them. Now many of them are lost beyond repair, many more are going.

Some of the canal system is being developed for pleasure cruising, for holidays. That is not what they were made for. A hundred years ago the canals were crowded with fleets of working boats, doing the needful job of carrying the heavy stuff of industry and agriculture all over the country. The Canal Families who peopled the barges were a very special society, unique unto themselves.

In the last century the canals were already threatened: the railways were taking over. In the end, this was to bring finish to the Canal Families' livelihood, and their particular and exclusive way of life.

Like all good boatmen, Joe Green came from a canal family. His father, brothers and sisters had long since left the canal; then he too was retired.

JOE GREEN I have twenty-one children, fifteen alive now. They was all born on the canal, out of me own earnings. I never had no family allowance for none of my children. Some of them was married when I had my last.

I had my first wife killed – left me with seven. She was stepping on the boat in Camphill locks, and her foot slipped and her dropped between the boat and the wall, and the boat swung around. Fractured two of her ribs and moved her heart. She lived about six hours after they fetched her out.

The barge-quarters were cramped, even for small families. Chocolate Charlie Atkins, working his boat on the Cheshire canals, raised a family of four on it.

CHOCOLATE CHARLIE The cabin was registered for so many, the proper register was for a man, wife and two children under twelve. Then you had to have another cabin on the front end of the boat and you were allowed to put two in there under twelve. I carried on for about four years and I got a cabin put on the other end of the boat then.

There were checkpoints everywhere, men from the council would come aboard to see that the cabins were clean, that all the children went to school.

JOE GREEN Used to go to schools at every place where we stopped at – Ellesmere Port, Birmingham, Brentford, Middlesex, all over the place. They used to have a card, what they call a travelling card. Any school used to take them in, just for half a day or a day when we stopped. All my children were scholared, what's alive, all the lot of them, sons and daughters.

JACK JAMES I've never been to a school, not inside of a school, no. But when we were kiddies, we could follow the horses along on the towpath, and sit on the cabin tops of the boats and watch the railway trucks go along.

We used to have a bit of slate and a bit of chalk and as the railway trucks were going along we'd take down the letters off the railway trucks, not knowing what it stood for. And we'd mark it down on a bit of paper and then take it in to the toll keeper. And we'd give him this bit of paper and say, what does this stand for? And he'd say: 'Ah, there you are, you've been chalking up the railway trucks again, come here, let me have a look at it.' He'd pick it up and say: 'Yes, you've got that right.' We only wanted telling once what it stood for, and we knew then what to put down if we wanted to mark Banbury down, Oxford, or Bedworth or any other place along the canal, see. We knew what to put.

Joe Skinner and his wife Rosie retired years ago, but still continued to live aboard their boat in Coventry. Joe never went to school, but Rosie did.

ROSIE SKINNER Yes, I went to school. Started when I was three and left when I was ten and a half.

It helped a lot when you could read and write. There was different people that would come and ask you to read letters and different things, see.

Letter-reading and writing was one of the jobs done by the toll-keepers along the canal locks. At Atherley near Wolverhampton the Shropshire Union Company had a toll-office at the junction with the Stafford and Worcester. In the 1920s the boatmen, after having their cargoes gauged, would collect their mail and get Sam Lomas the toll-keeper to read it out to them.

SAM LOMAS As well as ordinary letters, other letters I used to write and read for them was love letters. In those days the paper used to be what I call perfumed – smells very very scented. And of course the envelopes used to bear some kind of particular flower – either a wallflower or a little daffodil or a crocus. You could always tell whether it was from a boy or girl writing to their sweethearts. You used to see: 'Dear Lizzie, we're loading at Bramford for Birmingham, and I shall be there on such and such a date. Try to see me at the top of Gas Street or at the top of Dicton 3.'

JACK JAMES This toll-keeper, he used to keep a writing pad there, and envelope and a stamp if you hadn't got one. You hadn't got to bother, just tell him what you wanted to put in. He'd do all that, lovely letters he used to put together. We used to make it worth his while.

Jack Roberts was a boatman on the Shropshire Union, the old 'Shroppy', till the company folded in 1921. He traded the canals from the Mersey to the mountains of North Wales, from Ellesmere Port to Llangollen.

JACK ROBERTS I remember the canal as a boy of 9 or 10: the towing path was white and the grass was mowed, and there was flowers all the way from here to Llangollen – musk, yellow musk growing up the fronts, you see. And the bridges was whitened and the drawbridges were painted, number on each bridge. And that happened all the way through, from one end to the other.

SAM LOMAS When I first came here it was all commercial traffic. We were passing over a thousand commercial boats a week. In those days we'd neither room nor time for pleasure craft, and our approximate tonnage through a month was 36 thousand tons. That was import, export and internal traffic: coal, aluminium, copper, smelter, flour, sugar, all kinds. I remember, years later, when the last horse left the canal and all the boats were motor-propelled, I used to think, 'Thank God I wasn't born a boathorse.'

CHOCOLATE CHARLIE It was a hard life for a horse, because many a time he started at two in the morning and he wouldn't be finished until 10 or 11 o'clock the next night. He had to be at work all the while.

JOE SKINNER When I used to work I used to fancy mules to horses, they seemed more better to work on the towing path, more surefooted. We got stables a distance apart to put them. Oldsworth & Harroston, Nuneaton, Hawkesbury stop, Brinklow, Newbold, Ellmorton, Willowby, Branston, Bugby, Harford, Brisworth, Stoke, bottom of Stoke, Thruck Bridge, Cawsgrove, Linford & Finney.

JOE GREEN When you used to leave London they only used to give you so much money to carry you back to Birmingham. You got to pay your horse's stabling and pay tugging through the tunnels. Used to be eight bob for the pair of us for a tug to pull you through the tunnels. They used to give you £6 to start with. That would last you seven days when you got to Birmingham. Stabling the horse every night. You hadn't got much to throw away.

SAM LOMAS The boatman and his boss, they worked very harmoniously together. When he give him a load of cargo and tell him where it was for he could rely on him. And there were times when these loads were what we call 'fly loads'.

Boats with fly loads were lighter, carried less than twenty tons and worked day and night. The last fly boat to leave the Shropshire Union Canal was in 1919.

JACK ROBERTS There was a Trench fly, a Shrewsbury fly, Pottery fly. The Pottery fly was a four handed fly. The Shrewsbury fly was a three handed fly. The next one was the Brummagen fly. That was the main flyer of the canals, that was. That was two trips a week from Ellesmere Port to Birmingham, 84 miles each way. You only had one night a week in. That was Friday night because the Captain lived at Birmingham, and that was the only night, but it was a pleasure.

JOE GREEN I used to be handy with a flyboat. There used to be four of us on one flyboat. We used to work two and two, see. Right up to Trebor we used to go, right up to the bottom of the mountains. We used to take Cheshire farmers' stuff. You see there were no railways or nothing, no transport right up to Trebor and Llangollen and all those ports. It all had to go by water up there. There must have been 80 boats around there and they used to have 10 fly boats.

SAM LOMAS There was an old saying in them days: 'Nothing was ever too heavy and the weather was never too dark'. The only time as they were really stopped was when the canal was frozen up.

CHOCOLATE CHARLIE They used to have what they called an ice boat, and they would put horses on it and so many men to keep rocking it about, and then the horses would pull it and break the ice for us. I saw twenty-one horses on an ice boat a few years back.

There was a camaraderie among boatmen, but there was a great rivalry, to the point of violent quarrels. One point of difference was often the Distance Post. A certain distance from each lock both ways is a post, and the boat that is inside that, approaching the lock, had right of way. Because there were of course no referees, and boatmen never believed one another anyway, there was a lot of fighting.

JOE GREEN I hit a bloke one day. He went over the gate and down about forty steps. Split his head open right across. He was peaceless drunk with porter, drinking stout. He had to be taken to the hospital, had to pump stout off his stomach before they could operate on him to put stitches in his head.

There's 24 locks in Cheshire. I fought with every one of them locks. And my mother, she'd fight any man. It was all fight in them locks. The women used to say, 'I'll pull me bloody clogs off and pelt your bloody brains out'.

CHOCOLATE CHARLIE I wasn't much of a fighter. I used to talk my way out of it, because at the finishing you've got to meet the same people again. And while you're arguing the toss over a lock or anything like that the job is over and you're gone and your friends. But years back it used to be one of the biggest things on the canal.

The first time I got drunk was in New Year at a place called Norway Junction, and when we came out of there we went to friends house to call the New Year in, and then he fixed us up with some wine to about one o'clock in the morning. A friend of mine who was playing an accordion, he fell down and busted it, and I bent down to pick him up, and I fell with him. The fellow carried me to the boat, and I lost one of my clogs and I was striking matches at 8 o'clock in the morning trying to find it in daylight. I was that bad I couldn't load the boat. The captain came and he told me to get some tea without sugar and vinegar, that it would help. I was drunk for two days after and the only way I got sober was to drink seven pints. It was really a good Christmas, that was.

JACK ROBERTS The social life on the canal, you made your own. You would start from one end of the canal, you would say we'll go to so and so tonight – we would stop at the Truber and stable in there, pay the stabling, go and have a pint. And then of course a good natter, sometimes a song.

SAM LOMAS They used to call them ditties and make them up themselves. They were really good at this. There was an old ditty which they used to sing which was really good. 'Love is such a funny thing, it makes a man a fool.' The other favourite hymn is:

> 'Throw out the lifeline,
> Throw out the lifeline,
> Someone is sinking today.'

JOE GREEN Tell you a place there used to be a bit of sport with singing – Plants Lock, other side of Harecastle tunnel. In the Three Bells. We used to get in there at night, used to be the boatmen there with the curtain bonnets and long aprons, singing and dancing in the good old boatmen songs. There used to be blokes that could play a concertina. Finest music you can ever know is a concertina.

CHOCOLATE CHARLIE Today there's nothing travelling on the canal, only pleasure craft in the summer months. Might do a day or three days, you wouldn't see another working boat. The same when you tie up at night, you get to a place there used to be five or six boats tied up there, now there's weeks, months at a time and nobody ever goes there. There's only twelve of us, all the other firms are finished. Many a time now, I go a week, a fortnight just being on my own, just tie the boat up at night, switch the wireless on and that's all you'll hear till next morning. It's very, very quiet today. Pity, really.

To Paris - by Air!

Pilot in cockpit of a Handley Page Transport

Once upon a time there was this French daredevil Louis Blériot, who had the impertinent nerve to drive a heavier-than-air flying-machine across the Channel. That was in 1909.

Once upon a time, five years later, multitudes of young Europeans were learning to use these unnatural vehicles to make war with each other in the air, for the first time in history.

Once upon a time, in that same war, the guns and bombs borne by these aircraft became heavier, and the planes bigger. And then, quite suddenly, it all stopped. A lot of planes were left, and a lot of crews with nothing to do.

Unless, of course, someone could beat the swords into ploughshares. Since there was no longer any need to fly bombs across frontiers, what about people?

One company that got the message was Handley Page Ltd. of Cricklewood in North London, and an ex-RFC pilot called Robert McIntosh was with them at the time.

ROBERT MCINTOSH Handley Page 0/100 and the 0/400 were night bomber aircraft. In the front gunner's cockpit the Scarfe mounting was a mounting where you could swing your machine gun. It was taken out, and we had two passenger seats put there with small Avril windscreens, and then inside we had ten seats – one on each side – basket seats.

The Handley Page Transport was one of the first to get off the ground. But before anyone could fly commercially overseas there had to be Government permission, and pilots with civil licences. One air force pilot who went commercial was Jerry Shaw. He joined Aircraft Transport and Travel when in July 1919 the Press announced that civil aircraft were now allowed to fly 'beyond the confines of the United Kingdom'.

JERRY SHAW That was seen by Major Pilkington of the St Helens Glass Company, who had a very important meeting in Paris the following morning, about 11.30 I think, and he'd missed the night boat train. Having seen this advertisement he got in touch with our London office to see if he could charter a machine.

He most certainly could. He chartered a converted De Havilland light bomber. The gun-ring behind the pilot was taken out to make room for a passenger; the bomb-racks in the centre section were removed for a second passenger.

JERRY SHAW I was there at seven o'clock. Major Pilkington arrived a few minutes later in his raincoat and an umbrella, but although it was rather an historical moment, nobody was there to even take a photograph of him or the machine.

It's marked here in the logbook. The aircraft was an Airco 9, registered K.109. We took a hundred and sixty-five minutes, flying at two hundred feet. Hendon to Paris – Le Bourget. And in the remarks column – 'the first civil machine to the continent. Rain and low clouds all the way'. That's the only entry.

Six weeks later, on 25 August 1919, scheduled air services began. All the press and VIPs were at Hounslow Heath aerodrome watching Air Transport and Travel's planes taking off for Europe, with all the treatment of customs and passport control. It was the first daily scheduled international air service in the history of flight. Among the young men running the smaller aircraft to Paris was Alan Campbell-Orde.

ALAN CAMPBELL-ORDE I was only nineteen and three-quarters years of age when I got my civil licence to fly in this company. The war was over; we were still alive, which was something which surprised many of us I think. There weren't many jobs going around in those days, and we were delighted, I think, to get in on the ground floor.

These were the pioneers, the Francis Drakes of the skyways. Today your airline captain is in control of an enormous push-button computer system, a flying mathematical machine manipulated by complex instruments miles away. Not so in the 1920s. No radar, no guidance control, no ground-approach systems, no heating, no means of communication between the pilots and passengers. Every take-off on the two-and-a-half hours to Paris was an adventure.

ROBERT MCINTOSH We had a cruising speed of approximately 70 statute miles an hour. At Cricklewood aerodrome there was a hangar which ran on one side and hangars on the south side with a gap between – we used to aim for the gap and then we'd be over Cricklewood Broadway at about 30 feet doing about 50 miles an hour (with a ground speed indicated of 30 miles an hour) and the No '16' buses would go by below and we'd gradually climb, we'd hope, until we got above the Marble Arch about 500 feet then we would throttle back and then set course for Paris – we hoped!

Our height was confined to the height of the cloud. And very often we'd got into a valley – we'll say South Croydon. We knew we wanted to get South-East but the valley was going down South-West or due South and we couldn't get out of that valley. Although we knew we were going off course sometimes we'd carry on being pinned in the valley – you couldn't turn to get back, it was too narrow. And sometimes you'd hit the coast round about, let's say Bognor – and then you'd fly along the coast at about nought feet until you got to Dungeness – then you reset course again.

In the event of weather we used – the telephone was all we had – to phone through to the Tilbury Police. We would phone through and say er . . . 'Tilbury Police? I wonder if you could give me a weather report?' 'Yes, certainly sir, hold on.' He'd look out the window and he'd say, 'Oh, cloud about 500 feet sir, no rain, a bit chilly like.' You'd say, 'What's the forward vis?' 'I beg your pardon?' 'How far can you see?' And you'd distinctly hear him call to his mate on the gate – 'Harry, can you see the Fox and Dogs?' (It was a local pub.) If they answered yes, well, it was 2½ miles. And we used to go out due North to the Alexandra Palace and then about five minutes after we turned due East and then about ¼ hour later turned due South and hoped to hit the river around about Tilbury and follow the Thames down through the low country down to Lympne or to Dungeness.

ARTHUR WILCOCKSON If you did get lost, and I've done it frequently, coming from Cologne and that, and there was no way of finding out where you were. You had no direction finding, and you had to go down and read the name of the station and try and place yourself from there. We used to call that 'Flying by Bradshaw', after the railway timetable. It meant on the Paris run that you followed the railway from Redhill to Lympne – the main London line, when you crossed the Channel – the other side you picked up the railway at Etapes and you followed that down to Abbeville and from Abbeville to Paris you followed the main road.

I have taken four hours to do some of those trips. It sounds incredible today, but machines were only cruising 80/85 miles an hour and you've only got to have a strong headwind to push you right back.

In those days you did fly the aircraft by feel. The feel coming through the rudder bar and the stick and your other controls. You had your rudder which worked your direction. You had a wheel which was mounted on the control column. If you pushed your wheel forward you went down and if you pulled it back you went up.

ROBERT McINTOSH Our single-engine performance did not exist. You could say 20 secs. after an engine cut you were down on the deck. So if I saw a field into wind as I went along, and I thought that's a possible field I can get into; I found myself sub-consciously counting to myself – one, two, three and so on, until I saw another field, then I would restart counting. The whole idea was: if I had an engine go, I knew I could turn back and approximately after say twenty or thirty seconds that that field should be coming up. You bear in mind you're in an open cockpit, heavy rain, and you had to lift your goggles, and your vision was very limited.

It's rather difficult to explain, but when you're flying solo in those conditions you get in extreme turbulence, in addition to other things which make the control of the aircraft very difficult. You had to land into wind because we didn't have any brakes or flaps in those days, and once we had touched down, we used to switch off, then kind of waggle your ailerons to halt yourself. I remember once I sent my engineer back, going into a very small field, and when we touched down he was opening and closing the door to act as a brake.

I myself had eleven forced landings going to Paris. That was far from being the record. Engine trouble, water leaks, weather conditions – you'd get pinned down there. You'd land in the field and after about a half an hour it would lift a bit, and you'd carry on, and about another twenty-mile on the same thing would happen again.

The thing was: the mail had to get through. Under all circumstances the mail had to get through. I remember on one occasion I landed between Poix and Beauvais, and I was about 5 miles away from the nearest Post Office.

All I could do was to hire a farm horse, and I remember now sitting on this farm horse, frightened stiff, without any blind flying instruments, and I carried the mail 5 miles into Poix into the Post Office.

In the spring of 1920 the British aeroplane lines began transferring to Croydon, which was to be London's main airport for years. Then trouble came when foreign airlines started operating under heavy Government subsidy. The flight to Paris in those days was £20, but the French brought it down to £10. A. T. & T. had to shut down. Handley Page sacked almost all their pilots. Winston Churchill brought in the first subsidy, 25 per cent of load carried, but the little companies had to amalgamate. And then came Imperial Airways. But that is another story.

The Last of Feudalism

Horse team by Minterne pump

There is a way of life that belongs to the English past and still faintly haunts the English present; it diminishes over the years but here and there it endures. There was much in it that was bad, some of it was less so. Sometimes it is called Paternalism, or here and there Feudalism. It sustained the nobility in its day; now it embalms the remnants of the Ruling Class.

In Dorset is a small village called Minterne. Its life for generations had revolved around Minterne House, the 'seat', as they say, of the Digby family since the 18th Century. It followed the social pattern that evolved over the years, and 40 years ago began to fade.

In the 1920s the Digby home farm was managed by Mr and Mrs Batten.

MRS BATTEN They were really wonderful.

MR BATTEN Well, we was treated all right. We looked up to 'em and give 'em their place.

The 11th Baron Digby died in 1924; he was succeeded by his son, who was to run the estate as a modern farm. The 12th Baron went to Eton and Oxford and the Coldstream Guards and became Vice Lieutenant of Dorset, a J.P., and a farmer.

DIGBY I think we are the remnants of a feudal society here. Originally everyone was dependent on a feudal overlord. Aren't we still dependent on other people?

I think the things that make for happiness are an identity of purpose, enjoying the same sort of things, and feeling the same sort of achievement. Every time a good crop comes up everyone is pleased. And the harvest festival at the end of the season is an exciting time, everyone is relaxed and happy.

I think the good thing is to feel that other people are interested in you and what you're doing. I'm sure this is very true of my family who have always centred their whole life on this valley.

The Digbys first settled in the Minterne valley in 1765. It is three miles long and two miles wide, and it belongs, lock, stock and barrel to the Digbys.

DIGBY When Admiral Robert Digby first bought this estate he wrote in his diary: 'The estate is compact but naked, the trees not thriving and the house ill-contrived and ill-situated.' He set about rectifying this. I've got records of acorns which were put in the corners of fields, and now you see a tree a hundred and twenty feet tall.

Then his nephew, Admiral Henry Digby carried it on. And his son, the ninth baron, was a grandson of Tom Coke of Norfolk, so there was a big improvement of the land. Then came my grandfather, and my father. So that what you've got here is a valley which people say 'Wonderful, natural beauty'. In fact, of course, it's all man-made, by a whole series of people.

In these days big estates have to earn their keep. In the previous Lord Digby's day they did in fact exist solely for the enjoyment of the family. It was a way of life that had to be sustained by a regiment of retainers. Among them was Mrs Mitchell, who came to Minterne in 1914 as wife of the odd-job man.

MRS MITCHELL In the nursery there was two nurses on that top floor and a children's maid. There was the governess of course, then you come down to the kitchen, where there was a chef. And his wife, and another kitchen maid, and a scullery maid, and a between-maid, a still room maid, and then there was the head gardener and garden foreman and several gardeners under them. And then there was the coachman and the head groom and all the grooms under him. A butler, two footmen, hall boy, odd job man, four housemaids including the head housemaid. Lady's maid . . .

. . . and George King, the estate carpenter, who first came to Minterne as a boy of 11.

KING nursemaid and girls maid, and of course we had the laundry: there were four working in the laundry.

DIGBY Hilaire Belloc wrote: 'It is the duty of the wealthy man to provide employment for the artisan,' and these estates were built up in order to employ a large amount of labour, and – well, you were never out of work on a place like this, because something was found for you.

KING Many farmers went bankrupt, but you knew if you worked on an estate you were safe, and provided you behaved yourself and all that. Oh, absolute security, working on an estate.

MRS MITCHELL Well, I think we had more respect for one another than what we have today, you know. And I think we was more easily satisfied.

Of the 40 or so Minterne staff, only a handful remained. The Lakes, the Copps and the Curtises began work half a century ago.

MRS COPP We had very very little money. I used to come in and say: 'I've got 2d left this week, I'm well off.' I felt a millionaire nearly, I did truly, having 2d left after we'd paid everything.

There was six of us in family, and mum and dad, eight of us altogether, and we would have perhaps two slices cut for our tea, and there was no good asking for any more, because there was no more to be had.

During the first World War, I remember well the baker never come till half past eleven one night. Mother promised us, we all went to bed and when the baker come she would bring some up, at that hour of night.

Anybody that says them's the good old days, they can have them.

The Digby's passion, and leisure, for field sports involved a lot of servant-help. George Old was a woodman for 12 years, Lewis Squibb a footman whose family had been on the estate for three generations.

OLD He used to like his shooting all right. I mind down in one part of the cover I was shooting with Charlie Clack and we had to jump the brook. His Lordship was out in the cover in the shooting ride. Old Charlie was running back and forward. 'God,' he said, 'I can't jump.' 'What the hell's the matter with you, man?' said his Lordship, 'Jump' – Well, Charlie jumps right in the river. I pulled him up t'other side and Charlie marched on the rest of the day soaked to the skin. Afraid his Lordship was going to grumble to him again.

You might get a rabbit when you'd finished. Or you might not. All according to what sort of mood he was in. He was a real general on parade when he was shooting.

SQUIBB Yes, that he was.

DIGBY When I was being brought up I remember my mother thought she was economising very much with only sixteen indoor servants. Of course the discipline and the life below stairs was much more formal than anything we know.

MRS COPP Of course the butler was the big man wasn't he? His name was Butler, wasn't it? Mr Butler the butler. 'Sir' you had to call him.

MITCHELL Of course, the elder servants, the head housemaid and the butler and that sort of thing, they had the authority over them to keep the others just right.

MRS LAKE During the first world war I had to be in at half past eight every time I was out – every other Sunday.

FRED It was the war that changed it all.

KING I can remember before I came to Minterne when I was on another estate. When the girls met the Lady the girls curtsied, and the boy stood upright with his hands beside him and bowed. You was taught to do that.

MRS MITCHELL The Lord and Lady would visit the dairy, and the door steps would have to be whitened and while it was wet the crest would be stamped in the middle.

OLD I respected the man, and he had his honours, and I respected those honours. But why should you have to say good morning my lord, good evening my lord, afternoon my lord. And why should he call me Old and I have to call him 'My Lord'. Can you tell me that?

MRS BATTEN Lord and Lady Digby were so nice and so just. I mean you were very pleased to be working for them. They were so sweet, both of them, both her ladyship and his lordship – they were addressed as that, you see. I mean they were the Lord and Lady and you gave them their place naturally, because they were so sweet.

OLD The real truth about it, the only thing I didn't like was the domineeration. I'm not saying anything for his Lordship against him. Personally I suppose he was a gentleman and we always accepted that.

KING It was a close community. Everyone knew one another for years. Everyone got on with their job and was quite happy doing so. When the men left off work here, Saturday night, they'd walk to Cerne, down to Mrs Pawley's Elephant and Castle, to play bagatelle, and if they could win a pint of beer off one another it made their day. That was the life, those days.

MRS MITCHELL I like the old ways, you know, myself. There was a little village hall you know, where we used to have our whist drives and our dances, and sale of work and jumble sales, and that sort of thing. In the big house they did have a dance every other Friday. That was for the staff, and outside members if they cared to come.

MRS BATTEN We used to have the schottische and waltzes and one steps and quick steps, quadrilles and lancers, we always had to have those because of course they were a happy dance really, so many was in the sets that you was all happy together. And they always had a wonderful spread laid on for us all to have refreshments, you see. And they always said that they hoped we had a nice evening.

DIGBY Later on, when the cinema came in, my father used to show Charlie Chaplin films.

OLD The whole family was allowed to go, but let someone come in there and cough when the old man was working his box. He'd holler like hell: 'What's that man doing there?'

MRS CURTIS Remember when we went to Lord Digby's wedding, Mabel? That's the best day we ever had in our lives. We started from here about half past five, in our best clothes, didn't we, Fred?

Lord Digby gave us a marvellous lunch in a huge big restaurant, and we went on to this lovely wedding in St Margarets, Westminster.

MRS COPP Nothing to drink, only Champagne.

MRS CURTIS And Lord Digby came out and he waved us off, and he got up in the coach and he said to us 'Are we all here?' . . . and he ran along beside the coach you know didn't he, and he waved us 'bye 'bye . . . 'bye 'bye . . . marvellous he was . . . and he went straight to his club.

OLD I think those people in those days, if they were hiring you they were doing you a great honour, on top of wages, for hiring you. And they expected you to say 'Oh yes me lord, thank you me lord, I'll do that, me lord.' But I don't come to that, I never have.

KING You see, it's so drilled into us over the years that one automatically does it. Well, when one's in the Army one always salutes one's officers, doesn't one?

OLD Lord Digby was fair. He wouldn't have no hanky panky. If he wanted you, you had to be there at that moment, if you didn't, well, you could hear him all over the village. He paid, but he only paid what the agricultural structure was. Soon as ever the wages go up he might sack half a dozen blokes and bob's your uncle, you had to go.

LADY DIGBY I was talking to my son's Bailiff this morning – he was originally our cow-man down here. He puts it all down to my husband, that anyone who had anything to do with him was always happy.

OLD I covet no man's goods. But these kind of people those days had the money, and they had the working class, and they wanted to put the working class just to fit their convenience. And if they was doing that they thought they were doing you a good turn.

DIGBY Well, of course, inherited responsibility and wealth don't fit in with modern ideas, but I think one loses a certain amount. Of course I've been very lucky from that point of view. But if you don't have anyone inheriting wealth and being brought up in the sort of atmosphere that I've been brought up, you won't get people with a disinterested idea of public service. I do a lot of local government work, the same as my ancestors. We've been very well off, I think that to get people who have privileges, provided they stand up to the responsibilities, I personally don't think is such a bad thing. Most people wouldn't agree with me . . .

The First War in the Air

Duncan Grinnell-Milne

The 1914–18 World War was the first ever where battles were fought in the air. Imaginative writers like Verne and Wells had envisaged such a thing; in the First World War it came to pass; the heavier-than-air flying-machine became the warhorse of the new young cavaliers.

They rarely lived long. It was reckoned that the average life expectation of a pilot at the battlefront was three weeks.

Some survived. Two men who had the courage, skill, and luck to come out at the other end were Cecil Lewis and Duncan Grinnell-Milne.

GRINNELL-MILNE I began to fly at Shoreham in July 1915 and very exciting it was – a bit too exciting at times. In the first week of my arrival there were a few of us there – training pilots – and one day a very smart aircraft, a new BE2C, arrived from Farnborough and the pilot put down and had lunch with us. Afterwards, although it was a very blustery day, he decided to take off again. Of course we were delighted to see this expert pilot handling this brand-new machine.

He taxied down to the far end of the field and took off into wind. He was not much more than 50 to 100 feet up when we heard his engine beginning to starve. Now there's one obvious thing; if your engine begins to fail when you're taking off you carry straight on, you do not under any circumstances turn back. This fellow was so skilled and the aircraft so manoeuvrable that he thought he could do it. So he turned down wind and then the machine put its nose down and he disappeared behind the sheds, with the most awful crash.

As the plane began to burn the pilot got rather hot and jumped out with his clothing on fire. But the unfortunate passenger, poor chap, was wedged in the front seat and the flames got him completely. We could see him moving about a bit, and in front of our eyes there he was baked to death. And that was it. It did teach one the golden rule that with a failing engine you do not turn down wind.

LEWIS I went over to France with thirteen hours flying. It was considered a lot in those days, though in the Second War one couldn't go over with less than sixty. But they shipped me out with less than 13.

What one doesn't realise today was the extraordinary heavy rate of casualties. There was a continual stream of pilots going through, and the young pilot always went through the stage of starting, and hoping if he was lucky he'd get through his first month without being shot down. The raw pilots, fresh from England, hardly knowing their aeroplanes, were thrust into battle because there was great strain to keep the offensive going on the Somme.

They were faced with situations with which they couldn't cope and being shot down. The other way it happened was accidentally, because those people like ourselves in Number 3 Squadron who were flying very low, at 300 or 400 feet on contact patrol, were right in the trajectories of the gunfire, which was often an absolutely solid white blanket on the enemy side of the line, with the hundreds and hundreds of shells which were going over.

My own best friend and observer, while I was on leave, went up with another pilot on the dawn patrol and was just simply shot to bits by one of our own shells, direct hit. There was nothing left of them or the aeroplane. It was taking a heavy toll of our chaps.

And of course, if you happened to be up at 7000 or 8000 feet, there were the howitzer shells which were lobbed over like tennis balls. When you got to the top of the trajectory you could see them because they were pretty well motionless. You saw these great black porpoises of a 9-inch howitzer turning round slowly in the air and then going away, right down, and if you were quick you could follow it right down to the ground.

As the war went on aircraft design developed, became more sophisticated – and more difficult.

GRINNELL-MILNE Farnborough sent us out a thing which we called the pulpit, the B9. The designers had stuck in front of the propeller a little round box supported on a shaft, an extension of the main crankshaft at the engine. There were two cables that went out on the wings to prevent it twiddling round, and the observer sat in this thing in front with the propeller going round behind his head and, fine, he could shoot at any German aircraft he saw ahead of him, but he couldn't do much else. The terrible thing was that if you so much as did a bad landing and tipped the machine gently on to its nose, well, crunch, the observer was flattened.

LEWIS The machine I flew in France in 1916 when I really got down to business after a preliminary go-round with a B2C was a machine called the Morane Parasole, a French machine. It's the only case in the RAF, or the RFC rather, the only case where the wing was above the body. The body was underneath, rather like a stumpy end of a cigar, with a rotary engine in front, and over the top of this was this big flat wing braced with wires to a king post above and up to a king-post below. We sat underneath the wing. From the point of view of seeing the ground and doing observation with the infantry it was perfect.

Of course you realise that in these early aeroplanes you couldn't jolly well see below you at all. In an ordinary biplane the lower wing is underneath, so your forward view and downward view is restricted. The Parasole had a great advantage from that point of view.

I flew it right through the Somme battle for nine months. It was a terribly difficult aeroplane to fly because it had no tail. It only had a couple of elevators and these elevators were balanced about the fulcrum like a balanced rudder, you know. So they were terribly sensitive and as soon as you let go of the stick it shot forward on to the tank which was just in front of you, with a clonk, and the whole machine went straight down, you see, so you grabbed quickly and pulled it back again. You couldn't let it go for a second.

There was one great fight with the Richthoven Circus. We went into action eleven strong and five of us came back, having met about thirty-five of Richthoven's Circus, these red albatrosses. We met them at about 15,000 feet and we went on fighting down and down and down until I eventually finished up at 2000 feet with no more height left and the darkness coming down. But you know a fight in the air is so quick, it's almost impossible to recall it. All one can recall is a flash second when you saw a Hun in front of you and dived and squeezed your trigger to let the guns go, and then somebody else started up behind you. And you zoomed and pushed and lifted away to avoid the man who was at you, hoping that you'd got the chap below. Or you were circling tightly like this round and round each other in the hope that you could get the better of him, which was a question of machine performance and skill.

GRINNELL-MILNE They had a lot of clever tactics to outmanoeuvre us. If we were passing over the top of them they would literally stand on their tails underneath. A very striking manoeuvre. They hadn't got much zoom but they could pull their aircraft up and it was sufficiently light and the engine sufficiently powerful that for just a few seconds they could hang before stalling and get off a lot of useful shots underneath. Of course the answer to that was you didn't sit over them if you could help it. You just dived into them as hard as you could go and straight out the other side, and then you zoomed up to see what was happening.

LEWIS On the whole the real skill lay with the pilot, you know, how much he could get out of his aeroplane. And of course how long he would go before his guns jammed. Because the jamming gun was one of the great hazards which nobody ever thinks of now.

There was also in the SE5 this terrific thing with the Lewis gun up on the top of the wing, which had to be pulled down on a quadrant. And you were doing, say, 120 or more miles an hour and you had to take the drum off with your hand. The drum was about as big as a dinner plate. When you released the catch you had the whole weight of that with the force of a 120-mile-an-hour wind taking your arm back, you see, which it did very rapidly. You somehow or other got it down; then you had to get a heavy one up which was full of 120 rounds of ammunition, all in this wind, while God knows what was going on around you. It wasn't precisely an efficient form of fighting.

GRINNELL-MILNE I didn't like formation flying at low altitude; I didn't much care for it at any altitude, because one had to watch the leader all the time, which put one off. So as soon as I possibly could, I broke off, and I went off on my own.

I found one or two amusing little targets and I cruised about, and then I found something that I thought looked very tempting: I saw the flash of some guns going off and I thought well maybe that's a battery, I can drop a bomb on that. So I zoomed up as one was supposed to do, to gain a nice lot of height and then dived down, full out, and with both guns firing. Well I don't know what I hit or if something went off in the German battery underneath, but there was a most god-awful bang somewhere behind me and I went down vertically towards the earth. I suppose I had about 300 or 400 feet. I was going to hit the deck, full out, almost vertically.

The machine was coming out gradually of its own accord, it was a very nice stable machine, just a little bit of pull back and out she would come. But the ground was too close, and I knew I was going to hit it, and I did hit it. There were some more horrible noises, splintering and so on, and my undercarriage was wiped off, and the tip of the propeller blade as well. And then we staggered on into the air, at a very low speed indeed, almost stalling.

Well, there was nothing to do except sit there. I found the control stick was completely jammed. The aircraft was flying at half throttle, just about level, and then I looked round – I was horrified; one half of the tail it had gone completely, and was trailing behind on bracing wires. Even with a parachute I couldn't have done much getting out at about 100 feet from the ground. So on we went, and eventually from seeing Germans I began to see khaki uniforms. I just went on and throttled down, skidded along on my tummy and over she went. I don't know to this day what brought me out of it.

In June 1917 the bombing war spread to London. Cecil Lewis was recalled for defence duties over South-East England, both by day and night.

LEWIS We had no idea how to fly at night. I never dreamed of flying at night. You had to do something about it. So we got a torch from store, which had a little battery which I slung over my shoulder and a little tiny button which you clipped on the button of your coat, that was the light I had.

They had these things you've probably seen, half a two-gallon petrol can full of cotton waste and paraffin and just making a four-foot flame. Those were placed down the aerodrome in an 'L', so many along and one across the top. So then you just go along to the end, as far as I was concerned it was like going into the inside of a cow. I had no idea because there was no moon, you see. You didn't really know what you were in for. I remember taxying out and thinking: what the hell is going to happen now? I suppose I can keep straight as long as I can see the flare path. I can get up and then we'll see what it's like. I'd never been up at night before.

So I got to the end of the thing and pushed the throttle open slowly and she came away and lifted; and then I was in paradise. This wonderful, wonderful panorama of the night sky, and a plume of a train coming up from Southend or somewhere and the estuary of the Thames spread out in silver, under the starlight.

I carried on up and up and up till about 12,000 feet, and I kept on going up and down, up and down, up and down for two hours and never saw anything, and I did that month after month after month right through the winter of 1917–18 without ever seeing a single Hun.

GRINNELL-MILNE One of the last mornings of the war, it must have been the 8th of November, thereabouts – we were out early on patrol, and there was nothing up above, no German aircraft. After a while, as often did when there was nothing doing, towards the end I broke off with one or two other chaps. We turned out of formation, dived down to see what we could do on the ground.

Well, I came to a place where I could see some British troops lined up beyond the brow of a hill, beginning to advance. And over the brow of the hill were obviously the German positions. So I thought, this is where I join in. But there is nothing there. Positions were empty, the guns had gone. And then along the road I saw in the distance some Germans pushing a handcart or something. They were the last people of the retiring enemy. Then I saw lying across the road – I don't know why it particularly stuck in my mind, because I'd seen plenty of people killed and dying – but here lying across the road was just one German soldier. He'd been terribly wounded, probably from a shell splinter. It had taken all the flesh off his ribs, taken off his arm, he just lay there gasping. He was young, I could see that, and I suppose I must have been doing 150 miles an hour. He was moving, he was gasping, his leg was shifting up and down in the roadway and I could see his boot digging a little sort of trench in the mud. Where of course he was going to lie forever shortly afterwards. So I turned for home too and that evening I went on leave. It was the end for me.

LEWIS It took weeks to adjust to the fact that it was over and that one had come through. I was only 20 years old; I was sixteen and a half when I learned to fly. I was over the lines when I was 18. To find oneself with the whole of life before one, you know, and all the possibilities; it was an enormous sort of release. And yet I don't think one – one felt it that way. One was thinking, what next, what next? The future, always the future.

Zeppelins over England

The Coming of the Aerial "Baby-killers"

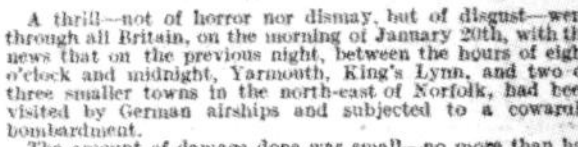

A thrill—not of horror nor dismay, but of disgust—went through all Britain, on the morning of January 20th, with the news that on the previous night, between the hours of eight o'clock and midnight, Yarmouth, King's Lynn, and two or three smaller towns in the north-east of Norfolk, had been visited by German airships and subjected to a cowardly bombardment.

The amount of damage done was small—no more than has happened often in a gas explosion—the loss of life slight; but the loathsome blood-mad fiends who could do this foul work and rejoice stirred every Briton's heart to sterner resolve to crush that degraded nation whose war methods are more savage than those of the lowest races known to anthropology.

Demented Germany is gloating over the proof that their Zeppelins can cross the North Sea and kill English children of four years old and English women of seventy. But British airmen, ten times more daring, have flown in daylight over long leagues of German soil and hovered over thickly-peopled German cities, and have dropped no bombs on civilians. Our Admiralty has warned Germany, however, that we can "take reprisals to any extent."

The Zeppelins braved three hundred miles of the North Sea to do—this! The ruined house at St. Peter's Plain, Yarmouth, and its wounded owner, Mr. Ellis.

Workmen removing what was left whole of the furniture from the house of Mr. Ellis at Yarmouth.

Page from *The War Illustrated,* January 1913

It was Germany that gave birth to the airship, the big dirigible buoyant gasbag, in the early years of the century. By 1914 dirigibles had flown more than 100,000 miles and carried more than 10,000 passengers without casualty. Sometimes it chanced that military men joined the crews for training.

Honours fell to the designer, who gave his name to the airship; the Count Ferdinand von Zeppelin. But he had always seen these great things as having a grander destiny than pleasure cruising. He saw them as flying warships. They would be a new and invincible arm to Germany's growing war machine. They would not carry passengers; they would carry bombs.

Some months after war came in 1914 the Kaiser finally agreed that the Zeppelins – as they were now called – were to be used against

Britain. A veteran of many of these raids was Kurt Dehn.

KURT DEHN We made a point of never approaching the coast until it was dark, because the communications system didn't exist in those days. So it was easily possible that nobody would know of the approach of a Zeppelin until he could hear the noise of the engine.

GEORGE HARRIS I thought to myself 'I don't know, I can hear something rhummn, rhumm, rhumm, rhumm, rhumm – like that you see'. And all about 2 or 3 seconds afterwards I could hear them coming nearer, and I thought to myself 'Well, I don't know. What is it? That's not an aeroplane,' I said to myself.

What George Harris of Great Yarmouth had heard was the approach of the first Zeppelin over England – No. L.3., commanded by Kapitän-Leutnant Johann Fritze. It was about eight in the evening of 19 January 1915.

GEORGE HARRIS I saw an object coming down, and all of a sudden I run towards my gal, what I was courting, and I said: 'I don't know, but I think that's coming this way.' Then there was this great explosion.

That was a bomb exploding harmlessly on a lawn in Norfolk Square. A second bomb fell in Crown Road, and failed to go off. A third fell near Gordon Terrace, doing little damage.

But then a fourth bomb fell beside St Peter's Church, and it killed two people; they were Miss Martha Taylor, aged 72, and Samuel Smith, a 53-year-old shoemaker. They were Britain's very first air-raid casualties.

That evening two young girls stayed indoors at 5, Drakes Buildings. They were Gladys and Kathleen Goudge – the tellers of Britain's first bomb-story.

GLADYS GOUDGE My mother went to what we called Daddy Goachers, on Victoria Road, to get the cough mixture, and she met Miss Taylor in there.

Miss Taylor lived at 2, Drakes Buildings, and when they came away, my mother said Miss Taylor walked a bit slow, she hurried on in front and I can remember this door being flung open and the windows coming in: my mother being thrown on to the couch.

Miss Taylor was unfortunate – she got killed on the road. So if they'd kept together my mother would have been killed and all.

KATHLEEN GOUDGE It happened just on the corner – just about a hundred yards away from here.

GLADYS GOUDGE That's where Mr Smith got killed too.

KATHLEEN GOUDGE Yes, Mr Smith had a cobblers shop just round the corner here and I suppose he came outside to see what was going on and he got killed.

GLADYS GOUDGE When you're children you soon get over it. Next morning we were fascinated to go through the rubbish of this opening to get out. You had to go in through the room, out the front, because there was too much debris.

While Great Yarmouth was being raided that January evening a second Zeppelin, the L.4., was making its way round the Norfolk coast dropping a few random bombs on the way. They caused no casualties. Eventually the commander, Kapitän-Leutnant Magnus von Platen, under the impression that he was over the mouth of the Humber, moved in to attack.

Olive Smith was spending a quiet evening at home in King's Lynn.

OLIVE SMITH We were told that there was a message through from Yarmouth to say the Zeppelins was on their way. They hadn't put the lights out here.

We were just sitting and talking. My father was reading and I was sewing or something. Then all at once there was this zoom – zoom – zoom – zoom – like that. And then the bang. I think there were three bombs dropped.

Leslie Bone and Reg Goat lived very near to where one of them fell.

LES BONE When that bomb dropped we all runned into the street. Proper calamity. Everybody came running across to each other's houses. The bed my sister and I were laid on was cut to ribbons and my father got us off just in time – else, that would've been our lot.

REG GOAT My father insisted we all sat under the dining-room table. He had the idea that we were being shelled from the river – no one thought anything about a raid from above. I heard that Percy Goat, who was a sort of second cousin, had been killed – and also a Mrs Gazeley. I believe her husband was in the forces at the time.

Private Gazeley had, in fact, been killed on the Western front only a few weeks earlier. Mrs Gazeley, Olive Smith's elder sister, was visiting friends on the night of the raid.

OLIVE SMITH She had been living at home since her husband was killed. My father went out to see if he could find her, but she wasn't of course in her own house and nobody didn't seem to know. They got the two people out that lived in the little house and took them to the hospital. My father found his way up to the hospital, and they wouldn't let him know whether she was there or not. When dawn began to come, he started pulling the debris about to see if he could find her. And he did find her. They said she died instantly.

A strong campaign was mounted for immediate counter-measures against this new menace from the air.

It was the Royal Navy's Air Service which at first took the brunt of the defence against the Zeppelins. Flying was something new for the Navy. One of their pilots was a young Flight Sub-Lieutenant, Gerard Fane.

GERARD FANE When the Zeppelins came, we had to concentrate on night flying. Originally, of course, flying at night was a sort of heroic business, and everybody thought you were marvellous. But it wasn't really as difficult as all that. But having gone up you had to do something when you got there.

We had a 12-bore paradox double-barrel shotgun with chain shot in one barrel and an incendiary bullet in the other. You went up with that in the cockpit with a 20-lb bomb in your lap. You had to be high enough to get over it you see. But they were quite hopeless, and nobody got really a chance to use them.

They tried some things called LePrieur rockets. You had four rockets on each side of the aeroplane, lashed on to the struts. The theory was you dived at the thing and pressed the button and the rockets did the rest, but, unfortunately, they'd only got a range of about 50 yards, and they used to go just ahead of the aeroplane when you pressed the button.

You very soon caught up with them and so they were quite useless. It would be much cheaper to ram the Zeppelin and get a posthumous V.C. or something rather than waste money on the rocket.

KURT DEHN In the Zeppelins, I don't think they even gave us a chair, because the 50 grams would have contributed towards the weight of another bomb. We were sitting on the chart table, if we were sitting at all.

Looking forward was one of the two N.C.O.s for navigation and steering. Then there was a commanding officer standing somewhere around.

You had to be very exact and knowledgeable to get the ship exactly over the target, and so many so-called targets were no targets. They thought they were over, say, the estuary of the Thames, and in reality they were near Portsmouth.

By the autumn of 1915 there had been nineteen Zeppelin raids –

four of them on London. Only St Pauls, Westminster Abbey and Buckingham Palace were forbidden targets.

Altogether 136 people had been killed in the random bombing of Britain. They were raids intended to bring Britain to her knees; but those who flew the Zeppelins knew that if they hit a town, let alone a specific target, it was more by luck than judgement.

KURT DEHN It was very difficult, unless it was a clear night, because the Thames can't be boarded up. So once we had the Thames, of course, we had London. It is all rubbish to say this was the so-and-so building and we dropped our bombs over that building. I never believed a word of that. You were happy enough if you found London, and you were even happier if you could drop your bombs and go home as soon as possible.

They weren't in much danger; the guns defending London were very few. In October 1915 seven aeroplanes were diverted from the European battle-front to operate from three make-shift airfields on the outskirts of the capital. There were only a handful of half-trained Royal Flying Corps pilots to fly them. One was eighteen-year-old John Slessor. He learned night-flying the hard way.

JOHN SLESSOR Purely by chance, one of my few claims to fame is that I, by luck, happened to be the first chap to intercept an enemy aircraft over England. But it wasn't a very effective interception.

It was the ordinary old stick and string aeroplane, no guns, of course, and the armament was a ridiculous Heath-Robinsonian device. You took a little bomb in your hand; you put it through a hole in the floor of the aeroplane and it lit an electric contact and as it dropped out came a bunch of fish-hooks, and these were supposed to stick in the skin of the Zeppelin, and it then burst into flames. The great snag of that was that it meant getting above the Zeppelin, and in those days it had a far higher rate of climb.

And I was sort of climbing to get my height and I suddenly saw this huge thing. It was enormous. Actually it was L. 15 commanded by a fellow called Briethaupt.

Some years afterwards I gave him a couple of gins in the R.A.F. Club, and we swapped lies, and he had been doing exactly what I thought. He was lying with his engine off to – listening, you see. Then he heard my engine. That was an extraordinary sight, because you suddenly saw a string of sparks come out of the lower engines of his ship. He didn't move forward much, but I remember being absolutely staggered by the angle at which he climbed. This huge bulk slowly tipped up, and just went *phrr* and left me standing.

While I'd been in the air, one of the half dozen anti-aircraft guns available had arrived on the airfield, believe it or not, with a searchlight. The fellow in charge of this thing thought it would be a help if he switched on the searchlight; which he did; bang in my eye – in the fog. By the grace of God I somehow or other just ran into the turnip field at one end of the stubble and broke various parts of the aeroplane.

KURT DEHN It was wonderful as long as you could fly in the dark. Then all of a sudden there would be searchlights far in the distance. They began searching for you, and then all of a sudden you were in the middle of the beam and there were six, seven, eight, twelve others focusing on you, and then the anti-aircraft would start shooting at you. You couldn't do much, because this six hundred feet long monster is not as moveable as a Fokker.

Yet during a year and a half of increasingly heavy raids, not one Zeppelin was brought down. Not until September 1916, when Germany mounted her biggest attack of the war, with 18 Zeppelins. Richard Ford saw one of them caught in the searchlights over North London.

RICHARD FORD I remember telling my father to come in the garden and have a look. We'd no sooner got out there than the local guns started blazing away. The shells never had any effect, except to drop shrapnel on our roofs, and knock a few slates off.

The Zeppelin was passing there and one could see it in the searchlights. 1500 feet up, 2000 maybe. I don't know.

I remember my father saying 'Good god, an aeroplane. How can he see to fly?' And this aeroplane started firing, coming from below.

It looked as though he was going right the way along the whole length of it. Nothing happened for a minute, and then the rear of the Zepp seemed to catch fire – just a slight glow, and then little bits began to drop off. The Zepp still kept going. It seemed a long time before it really burst into flames.

Edward Mills was with a contingent of Royal Flying Corps mechanics called out on alert in Woodford, Essex.

EDWARD MILLS Then it disappeared. It went into a small cloud and suddenly the cloud started getting red. We realised then that the Zepp was on fire.

There wasn't a soul about in the streets. But directly that Zepp caught fire I never heard anything like it. The back gardens and windows and streets – people shouting and cheering just like as if you were at a big gathering. Remarkable.

RICHARD FORD My father said 'I should think it's just about Enfield'. I said 'Can I pop on my bike and go and find where it is?' He said 'Well, yes, tomorrow's Sunday, so off you go'. I got my bicycle out and off I pedalled, three miles to Enfield. No sign of it. Saw a glow in the sky somewhere and one or two people knocking around. Eventually found myself at Cuffley, where there was this blazing Zepp in the field – on the top of the hill.

They erected ropes all round to try and stop people going in, but I was on the inside of it. I was looking, naturally, for souvenirs. I couldn't get near the thing for the heat. I kicked something on the ground, picked it up, dropped it: it was too hot. It was, strange to say, the broken-off hilt of a sword.

That Sunday thousands came searching the area for the smallest fragment. For well over a year the Press had called for the destruction of the German 'baby-killers', and now at last there had been retribution.

Newspapermen now saw that the remains appeared to be little more than tangled wire. 'Germany Running Short of Metal', they wrote triumphantly. In fact this airship was a new type with a wooden frame and was not from the regular Zeppelin factory at all. Still, Press photographers had a field day.

EDWARD MILLS Well, we had to go over there, quite a squad of us. We had a trailer draped in black, and the coffins put all along the trailer. The Zepp commander was on a smaller trailer.

We had to lay the coffins all in a row and they had a tremendous big grave dug. Big oblong grave about 4 to 5 feet deep. They had sort of steps to go down to it and the Zepp commander we buried in a separate grave at the top of the large grave.

One irate lady, she had an egg in her hand and she let fly at the coffin, and it hit the side of the coffin and splashed all over.

From then on the casualties among these vast airships grew almost weekly, as defensive techniques improved. Zeppelin crews came to realise that a sortie over England was likely to end in destruction.

KURT DEHN Whenever I think of Zeppelins, I think of that moment of sunset when you realised in your thoughts – is it now goodbye sun, or is it au revoir? The alternative was: you would either sit in your mess room next morning and have your eggs and bacon, or your bones would be lying in one of the fields of England.

In November 1916 Flight Lieut. Egbert Cadbury intercepted one Zeppelin over the Norfolk coast returning from a raid on the

Midlands. In a nearby plane Sub-Lieutenant Fane got close enough to attack.

FANE I think this one had been somewhere near Coventry, so we knew it was coming but on an easterly course and one was able to pick it up somewhere off the coast of Yarmouth. Egbert Cadbury also picked it up at the same time. Cadbury actually started shooting before I did.

I went in close, about 30 or 40 feet underneath it. Then my gun jammed, so I had to clear off and go over the top to try and bomb it, and by the time I'd got there it was well on fire. The heat was terrific when it really got going. It wasn't a very cheerful sight. All right, so we were there to destroy it and we had destroyed it, but it wasn't a thing you sort of cheered about too much.

And so it went on. There was a final, seemingly suicidal gesture by Peter Strasse, Chief of German Airships. On 5 August 1918 he led a raid of three ships in the enormous new L.70, almost incredibly crossing the English coast before it was fully dark. At once there was a scramble by every available plane from Yarmouth. Egbert Cadbury got off first in a DH.4 and shot down the L.70. Stanley Fetherston had taken off in a flying-boat and was still climbing.

STANLEY FETHERSTON There was a layer of cloud, and it became quite a heavy rainstorm. I was at about 10 or 12 thousand feet and the L.70 was about 18,000 feet. I saw what I thought was a petrol tank on fire. I think they must have been nearly finished before that raid, otherwise I don't understand why Peter Strasse came. I think it was a sort of final gesture. And, of course, it didn't come off. There was no other attempt.

The Zeppelins had raided Britain on 51 nights, and dropped some 6000 bombs. Forty per cent of the German crews were killed.

In the four years of that war more than 500 civilians were killed by Zeppelin bombs.

Across the Channel a million British soldiers had died.

Two Abandoned Islands

Leaving St Kilda

ONE: ST KILDA

'We the undersigned, the natives of St Kilda, hereby respectfully pray and petition H.M. Government to assist us all to leave the island this year, and to find homes and occupations for us on the mainland . . .'

(From the petition by the islanders of St Kilda to the Rt. Hon. W. Adamson, Assistant Secretary of State for Scotland, 10 May 1930.)

On 29 August 1930 the most isolated community in the British Isles became news for the first time in its history. St Kilda is 110 miles from the Scottish mainland. Cut off and ignored for generations, its tiny population had struggled to survive in impossible conditions. Finally they had surrendered. At their request, St Kilda was evacuated. The men and women were to begin life again in the Scottish Highlands.

Neil Ferguson was 30 when his island was abandoned.

NEIL FERGUSON There was 150 of us on St Kilda, and it was going down and down, till it came down to 36. There wasn't enough to man the boats. All had to clear out.

Lachland MacDonald was 24 when the end came.

LACHLAND MACDONALD We were getting a newspaper maybe only once a month in the wintertime. You didn't know what was going on in the outside world at all.

Fifty miles west of the Outer Hebrides, St Kilda is a group of little islands: Dun, Soay, Boreray and Hirta. Only the biggest, Hirta, has ever been inhabited. Yet even Hirta is less than nine miles long and a mile or so wide. For all but a few summer months the place was almost wholly out of touch with anywhere. For the rest of the year the place was sealed off by storms and gales.

The only outsiders to share this isolation were a nurse and a missionary. Miss Mary Cameron was the missionary's daughter; she had been on St Kilda since 1919.

MARY CAMERON They were people of very strong character, kind and hospitable folk. Their lives were upright in every way. There was no insobriety or anything like that. No dishonesty. People didn't lock their doors. They would be coming in and out of each other's houses at any time, and the people themselves were just like one family. What was one family's sorrow or joy was sorrow or joy to the rest.

They lived in one row of 16 houses, each one the same as the next. There was no head of the island, but there was an informal 'parliament' where decisions were made by the men. The only outside authority was the United Free Church of Scotland.

NEIL FERGUSON If you didn't go to Church, first thing on a Monday they would come and see what was wrong, and if you weren't badly you got a telling off. You had to go. You had to go to Church.

Isolated as they were from the mainland, the islanders relied for their living on the birds nesting on the towering cliffs – the gannet, puffin and fulmar. Fowling had been their occupation for centuries, starting in April with the gannet. The men would row out in a small boat to the neighbouring stacks and risk the steep crags.

LACHLAND MACDONALD We went in a wee boat, and the swell was coming in. It's no easy to get to the land. But there was a pin put on the rock there and you'd throw the rope over it, so when you get it up on that pin the first fella would jump out.

We had to climb it, climb it, and that's no easy climb if the weather was wet. Oh, you had to go ashore and climb to the very top of the stack.

DONALD GILLIES You had to catch the birds by the head, whip back and off it went. There was a knack in it. Oh, you had to be up to it or else he would get you. Start catching them and killing them, and throwing them below into the water below and the folk in the small boat was collecting them.

MARY CAMERON There were sometimes fatal accidents. To fall down the cliff was a dreadful thing, because there was no hope of anybody being rescued.

NEIL FERGUSON Nobody could swim. So, you can't swim, you have to drown.

The climax of the year was the fulmar harvest. To the islanders the fulmar was the most important bird – its meat their main source of food, its oil their fuel. Thousands were killed on the narrow ledges of the cliffs.

DONALD GILLIES You left them to the end of August and they were all flying away. You had to clean them and salt them and store them for your feed during the winter.

You could catch three or four hundred of them at a time and take them home. So that's the way they were catching the birds, they were.

MARY CAMERON They'd been bred to it for generations, from childhood. Even the little boys wanted to be let down the cliffs. I've seen a little boy of ten being lowered down like that bringing up his fulmars with the rest.

But it wasn't only small boys who were lowered down the cliffs. Flora Craig was six when, with an uncle, she tried catching her first fulmar.

FLORA CRAIG We saw a fulmar on a nest there, so he thought 'How would you like to go down?' Well, I didn't fancy it very good, but I thought 'Well you should, really.' So he put a rope round my waist and he sort of flung me down, and I landed beside the fulmar and it was sort of making funny noises. I discovered after it was trying to bring up oil, if they're angry and that they seem to spit up oil at you. It happened to turn away and I just grabbed it by the back of the neck. I was that proud.

NEIL FERGUSON Everybody helped each other. You ran short of anything, if your neighbour had it you would get it. That's how it went on.

FLORA CRAIG Mother had four of us and she really had to work hard. But they were quite good at helping one another on the island. Most of the people had sheep and cattle, and you used to milk your own cows.

DONALD GILLIES The winter time was for carding and spinning and weaving and, oh, what-not, without a halt. That was going on from day to day, from week to week. Takes a long time to spin, to make the wool into thread with a spinning wheel. Carding it, combing it. Different things to everything.

LACHLAND MACDONALD So that's the way you were living on St Kilda. Then you were up as soon as it was daybreak and doing something. There was no rest there. It's very little money you had. Mostly in exchange for your food you were doing it.

NEIL FERGUSON You used to kill a sheep maybe a week, and what you didn't use you would just throw away. There was no sale of lambs or sheep. You had just what you used yourself – you couldn't get it to the mainland. Same with the fish. Supposing you get a big halibut, maybe, you'd share it out to anybody who wanted it, and throw the rest to the birds. That was the trouble, there was no market for anything there.

In the summer, steamship companies in Glasgow advertised a journey to 'the romantic Western Isles and lone St Kilda'. And each year a few tourists undertook the 10-day voyage. To the islanders who ferried them ashore it was a chance to sell souvenirs. To the tourists stepping ashore on St Kilda it was like visiting a zoo. They were often inquisitive and patronising.

FLORA CRAIG In St Kilda you only got sweets in the summertime from the tourists. We used to try and sell socks and gloves; and sometimes we were lucky, got sweets from them.

DONALD GILLIES These socks were made of the St Kilda wool. They're nice and soft. They'll be up to forty years old. Last yet another while, I expect.

The summer also brought a visiting Minister who gave Communion and carried out any baptism or marriage services – which the resident missionary was not eligible to do.

The last wedding on St Kilda was Neil Ferguson's in August 1925.

NEIL FERGUSON When anybody got married, they all came to the one house and had a good feast and all that and maybe a bottle or two of whisky and they killed a sheep or two. All the women had to bake scones and oatcakes and things. There was no shops anywhere. If you wanted any fancy stuff you had to get it through the mail, and it might be lying in the post office maybe for a month or two and all rotten when you got it.

But work was never far away, and in summer a number of the men would be taken by boat to the uninhabited island of Boreray to shear the sheep.

DONALD GILLIES The boat would go back. You were left there for a week or ten days according to the weather.

If the men on Boreray wanted to contact the main island they had a series of signals, made by marks cut into the turf, to say they were ready to return, whether somebody had fallen ill, and another if somebody had died.

FLORA CRAIG They knew it was a death on this island. So the wee boat went away for them and when it did come back all the womenfolk were down on the pier. They just didn't know who it was, and once it was my father, died with appendix. My mother was left with four of us.

MARY CAMERON It was such a small community, and everybody was closely related to everybody else. In the year of the General Strike in 1926 we had a severe epidemic of influenza. Four of the older people died in one week. It was a terrible blow for such a small community.

In the seven years Miss Cameron had been on the island the population had fallen from 74 to 50. In the next four years it was to drop even further, to 36.

In 1928 Miss Williamina Barclay took over as resident nurse on St Kilda.

MISS BARCLAY During the winter we'd only mail once in a blue moon, because the trawlers couldn't come in for the storms. The result is the Department of Health had only four sailings in the year. The eight months we were on our own.

DONALD GILLIES You might get a trawler or one of these fishing boats that would bring you a message and the mail maybe at times, but the regulars were finished from May to August and that's you locked out.

NEIL FERGUSON I was supposed to be the postman. The year before we left the last mail we got was in August. It was March before we got the next.

The last winter was the worst ever. For months there had been no contact with the mainland, and food was running out. Finally the islanders persuaded the missionary to write to the Prime Minster, Ramsay MacDonald. 'We are now twelve weeks without news or relief supplies. For weeks almost all of us have been without sugar or potatoes. Paraffin oil is also running short when we most require it for light to work our looms in the making of Highland tweed.'

MISS BARCLAY The missionary was the teacher. While he was a good Christian man, he hadn't the ability to teach them, you know, as they ought to be taught. When they grew up a bit there was nothing for it but for them to leave, and I thought they would be better to be educated in Glasgow, or wherever.

Finally, I said to them 'Now, you're to think over this – you're to pray over it and make up your minds and don't talk about it for a week. And I'll not talk about it either.' But before I got out of the house they're all on their feet and I was told that they would be glad to see the children on the mainland and being brought up as I had been brought up. That was the beginning of the end. They petitioned the Government.

My urgent point was that if they came off, they were to go to suitable homes. And also they weren't to all live in a row as they were living in St Kilda. They were to become individuals.

The Under Secretary of State for Scotland visited St Kilda and it was agreed that work and homes would be found for the islanders with the Forestry Commission in different parts of Scotland.

DONALD GILLIES Ah well, we made up our minds to get out of it, that was the only cure. We knew from the beginning of April it was going to happen before the end of the season, so it did happen then.

On 27 August 1930 the *Dunara Castle* sailed into Village Bay to collect the sheep and heavy furniture. On 28 August the HMS *Harebell* arrived, to take the islanders.

NEIL FERGUSON We had a service in the church the day before we left, and most of the Bibles were left in the church.

DONALD GILLIES It was one continual work all the day, getting furniture down on your back to the pier, transferred with a small boat out to the *Harebell*. This was going on till it got dark, and in the early morning we started again.

NEIL FERGUSON We left the lines to rot, all the lines and fishing gear, all the looms and that. We took the spinning wheels. Took the dishes and things like that.

And we went away at nine o'clock, that was the time they sent for us. The *Harebell* was leaving at nine, if you weren't on the boat then you were left there yourself, Robinson Crusoe. Aye.

FLORA CRAIG It was a lovely day, and I can remember us being on the boat and looking back and we were crying because it looked so nice, and all the chimneys, the smoke out of all the chimneys and the sea so nice and clear, it was really a lovely day.

DONALD GILLIES Yes, oh yes. I was looking at it till the last sight I could see. Yes. They came to Barra Head, they came to St Kilda round Barra Head. Aye. It was sad in a way but in another way it was quite good, what did happen.

TWO: ALDERNEY

June 1940 and the advancing Germans were pouring down the coast of Normandy. For the inhabitants of Alderney in the Channel Islands they were getting too close. Alderney is only 8 miles from the mainland of France. It is the nearest of the Channel Islands, and one of the smallest, just 3 miles long.

Still living there, just after Dunkirk, were 1500 people. But on Sunday, 23 June 1940, they left. A week later the Germans moved in, garrisoned the island, and held it for five years.

Even today, years later, the islanders who returned remember the time they left their homes behind. Like Mrs Duplain, who for years had kept the ironmonger's shop with her husband Ralph. Or Babs Tinson whose father had kept the pub, the Campania. Cath Soffe whose family run the bakery. Or her sister Lilian Audoire, the island's postmistress.

They had to make this huge decision.

CATH SOFFE This is the position. We either all go, or all stay and face it together. It is no good half going and half staying, so the majority said 'go' and that was it.

MRS DUPLAIN You can imagine how they felt. Some in tears, some asking silly questions, most went home and packed what they intended to take, the rest they just buried in the garden.

The afternoon after this the town was very quiet. We all wondered what was happening. We had no idea the boats would be arriving in the morning.

CATH SOFFE Sunday morning at 7 o'clock we were all awakened with the church bell going full belt, so this was it, up, wash, dress and away to the harbour.

LILIAN AUDOIRE Everyone took their pets to be destroyed. It was heartbreaking, it really was. You just couldn't leave animals locked up; you couldn't take them, so something had to be done.

It was chaotic. Anyone who had a car went to fetch people who lived outside the town, because although the church bells were pretty loud quite a number of them didn't know that we were going.

MRS DUPLAIN Dead silence, no panic, no scenes of any description. The Officers of the ships were there with revolvers in their belts. Apparently they expected panic stations.

Five colliers, manned by the Navy, arrived at eight in the morning, Sunday, 23 June. By ten o'clock they were loaded and away with the help of Alderney's Trinity House pilot – Nick Allen.

NICK ALLEN I was the last man away. There were cattle straying all over the place, some were right down at the end of that breakwater, you know, just saying goodbye to us as we were going. All the horses were roaming around. Dead as a doornail it were.

LOUIS JEAN I would have liked to have fought for the island. If the island should have been lost in battle, it would have been a different thing for me.

CATH SOFFE When we got to Weymouth, someone said 'There's an interpreter here'. I think they must have thought that we had come from outer space or something.

LILIAN AUDOIRE We were all herded into a large cinema. Quite a lot of people were having a weep. We had some friends who found accommodation for us. I think the enormity of the whole thing hit us when we were asked to sign the Visitors Book. We suddenly realised for the first time that we were refugees. We literally had no home, no address, nothing.

Some with relatives in Britain were allowed to join them and were soon scattered all over the country. Those with no one were sent up to Scotland.

MRS DUPLAIN They were supposed to have gone to Lancashire really. They were taken to Glasgow, where nothing was ready for them. I suppose one had to put up with these things.

HENRY ALLEN I went in a Foundry at first, I was three years in that Foundry. I liked it all right. I had £9.16 on the night shift, £8.16 on the day, that was for 12 hours a day. We had to work for our money.

CATH SOFFE We were in the town one day, we saw a placard, outside one of the cinemas 'HMS *Rodney* shells Alderney'. We couldn't get in quickly enough.

The *Rodney's* job was to silence the German guns that could threaten the Cherbourg crossing. The islanders watching the newsreel saw the shells being loaded into the guns, and wondered what on earth they would do to their homes. *Rodney* was sending 75 one-ton rounds lobbed over the Cherbourg peninsula to Alderney, 17 miles away.

As it turned out those 16-inch guns did little damage, and in fact the German garrison had a pretty quiet war. In May 1945 they surrendered the island that had been more than a garrison; it was also a prison. One of the first islanders home was Nick Allen.

NICK ALLEN It was pathetic. When I came back here with the Navy to reoccupy the island, to see the Russians, Georgians, French, a mixture of all kinds. Masses of them in a poor looking state. They were marched down the jetty, sprayed, powdered, before we transported them away. Horrible to look at, almost like animals I suppose. There were Germans everywhere, and the slave labourers.

To help the reconstruction of the island the British brought in German prisoners of war from the other Channel Islands, and they worked alongside the people of Alderney rebuilding the place. One of them was Karl Curth, who was brought over and stayed to make Alderney his home.

KARL CURTH At first sight all we could see was barbed wire, steel posts, trenches, concrete bunkers, tank traps, trenches; whatever it is you need for a fortress, it was here. I suppose they thought it was part of Great Britain and we can say, well, at least we have got something occupied of Great Britain.

MRS DUPLAIN We were due to come back on the 6th of March. We made for Southampton, and when we got there we met people from the island who had come from all parts of the country, and everybody had chickens, fowls, a puppy, cats, dogs, pigeons, everything you could think of.

LILIAN AUDOIRE I came back for the first time in June 1946, by mail boat, got up when we were off the Casquettes Lighthouse. You get a good view of Alderney from there. I shall never forget the feeling of seeing it, after 6½ years and not hearing anything, it didn't seem possible that it was still there, but it was.

MRS DUPLAIN Having left everything, we naturally thought we were coming back and find it all there. I don't know why we did, but we did. There was nothing.

LILIAN AUDOIRE There were whole streets where the roofs had gone, all timber was stripped from them. Apparently during the best part of a year, the island had been blockaded, so the Germans had been forced to burn every bit of wood they could lay their hands on, and the atmosphere was eerie. There were about four concentration camps. There was a funny sort of smell which was very odd indeed.

MRS DUPLAIN They should have kept the prisoners to clean this all up and do the scrubbing, not us. However, we did it and we cried and we scrubbed and we said 'Well, I suppose it will be worthwhile'.

JACK HAMMOND Anything you wanted, it was no good trying to ask the civil authorities, Home Office representatives then, but you only had to ask a German, and you would get anything you wanted.

KARL CURTH We got very well on with them. We done odd jobs for them, helped them with moving things you know, because there was absolutely nothing for them to come to except four walls.

DICK ALLEN We found the Germans would help us do anything. Build walls, paint. We weren't allowed to pay them, but we would give them a packet of cigarettes.

KARL CURTH Of course that was a bit of a business then. It started from, say 20 cigarettes, 50 cigarettes, and it got it went up to a hundred and even more.

DICK ALLEN If they were working in your house for a few days they would arrive with a little bunch of wild flowers for your wife. They always seemed to want to make amends for what they had done.

JACK HAMMOND I used to do quite a bit of trade with the Germans. One day they asked me for 2 dozen Pony ale, that's small bottles, you see. I told them that it would cost a lot of money. I could speak their language cause I'd been a prisoner in Germany in the First World War, so he said 'No, we got no money, but I'd pay you Monday'. So I said 'But if you've no money how are you going to pay me?' He was going to bring a carpet, you see, so I said 'Why wait to Monday?' Well, he was going to take the carpet out of the Church to pay me for the Pony ale.

MRS DUPLAIN Our own troops, it is shocking to have to say it, but they did the looting, not the Germans. They were having all these cases made at the works where the Germans were working, so it is quite obvious what they had in all these cases.

BABS TINSON They thought they were taking them from the Germans. It wasn't until I said to them 'You are not robbing the Germans, you are robbing those people here.' The Alderney people were coming back. They thought they were being smart and getting it through Jerry.

MRS DUPLAIN Of course there were thousands of Russian slave workers here. We fortunately didn't see what happened to them all, but I did see photographs of where they were buried in the sea walls, and all the pitted marks in the walls apparently are where they used to machine gun them.

LILIAN AUDOIRE I think that a lot has been exaggerated of what went on here, but there's no doubt that some pretty awful things did happen.

BABS TINSON But the Germans did a lot of good to Alderney, as well you know. At least we had piped water when we got back, we had electricity laid on in practically every house. We hadn't that when we left. They did a lot of damage, they did a lot of bad things, but one or two things, I mean, really worked out well.

I have learned one thing, anyway, never put a lot of faith in anything you possess, because you can lose it so quickly.

An English Nurse with the Tsar's Army

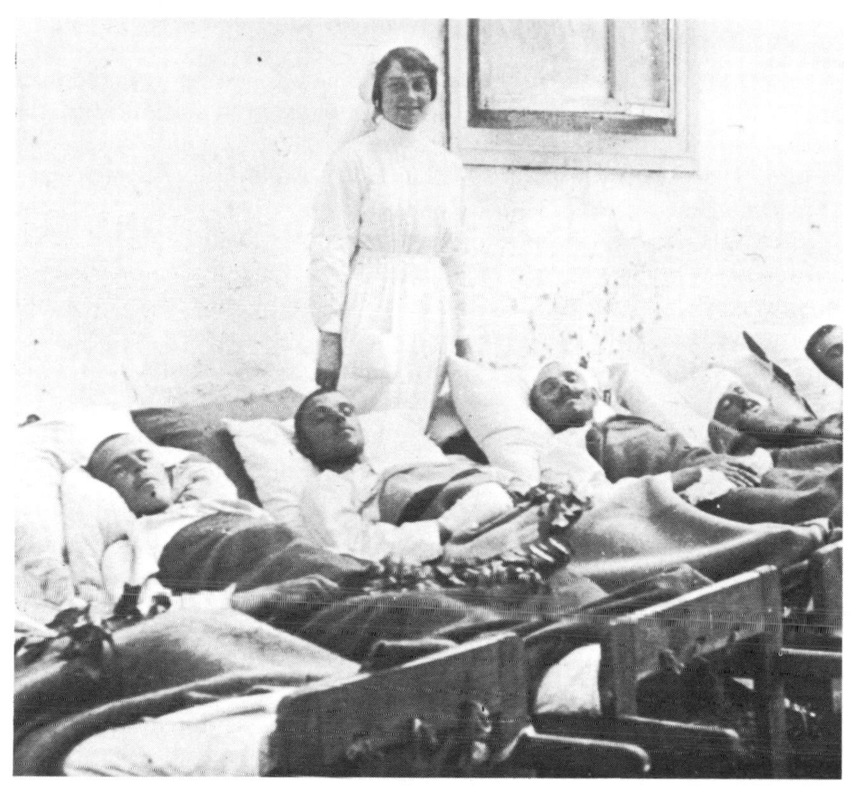

Florence Farmborough with wounded soldiers at the front

In 1914, Russia was the last of the great feudal empires, a vast land where dwelt 170 million people, most of them profoundly poor, and a few immensely rich. And every one of them was the property of one man: Nicolas II, Tsar of all the Russians, a monarch of almost medieval splendour.

And in three years it was all gone: the Tsar, the Court, the power, all swept away by a new order that claimed to give a voice to the speechless, and came to be called Communism. But that was still to come.

There was another image of all this ostentatious majesty, one which few strangers ever saw. But one witness did see a telling aspect of the Tsarist days – and a strangely improbable witness too: a young and very proper English girl from the Home Counties, a certain Florence Farmborough, a governess.

One day in Moscow in 1914 she saw the Tsar of all the Russias in procession close by.

FLORENCE FARMBOROUGH And just as he was passing us an old man suddenly emerged from under the ropes, ran across in a crouching position to the platform and held out a paper to the Tsar. The Tsar didn't even look at him. There was a whispering: 'What is it?' 'A nihilist', 'An anarchist'. No, just a peasant with a petition to the Little Father the Tsar, to grant special rights to the downcast peasantry. But why had not the Tsar answered? Why had he not even made a movement to show that he acknowledged his presence? Because he would not be allowed to. He could not touch or accept any touch from his citizens. At home we discussed what would happen to the man. They said, probably exile for life.

Home, at that time, was the country house outside Moscow of a rich heart-surgeon whose daughters Miss Farmborough was teaching English. She did, to be sure, witness the coming revolution from a special point of view; she shared the conservative and insulated values of the people of privilege among whom she had been living for several years.

But what was more, she was a photographer, and a very good one. Florence Farmborough took many pictures recording the country estate where she lived and the ample life that was not to last much longer.

In 1914 came the war between Russia and Germany and Austria, and the bell tolled, though nobody heard it then.

Nevertheless, for Miss Farmborough life changed completely. The pleasant role of the English governess in peace became the life of a woman at war. Florence Farmborough decided to stay in the Russia she had come to love, and train as a nurse.

This young English girl joined the staff of a new military hospital in Moscow – and for the first time encountered something familiar enough in Russia, which is death. It came to her in the end of a soldier she had befriended. There were to be many more, but the first is always the worst.

FLORENCE FARMBOROUGH One morning I went back to our Red Cross Hospital for the wounded soldiers, and I met the night nurse and she said: 'Vasiliy has died'. I went straight to the mortuary, and then I realised that death is very quiet, very silent and very remote. And because of its quietness and silence and remoteness I got frightened, I know I went out quickly and shut the door.

Florence Farmborough was now emotionally committed; she had to help, and to get to the front she had to qualify as a Red Cross Nurse, which she did, joining a Field Unit in Moscow.

The North West Front was a 5-day journey from Moscow. The Russian Army was huge, hopeless, strong, badly trained, impossibly equipped and disastrously led. It faced the most efficient and sophisticated military machine, possibly, in the world. But the Russians were brave, and they were also numerous.

In the Field Unit Nurse Farmborough met two colleagues who were to be at her side until the end: Mamasha, the housekeeping sister of the unit, and Annushka, the youngest nurse of the group.

Miss Farmborough found that the Front was not at all what she had expected.

FLORENCE FARMBOROUGH Do you know, I was very upset there was so little work. I remember saying to Mamasha one day: 'Mamasha, if this is going on all the time I might as well be in a hospital in Moscow'. And she said: 'What do you want? Do you want a massacre of soldiers? You want them coming in, terribly wounded, so that you can nurse and bandage them?' I said: 'Mamasha no, that's the last thing I want. But I want really hard work.' Mamasha said: 'The worst is still to be. Wait, and be patient.'

We didn't have long to wait. The 1915 offensive was just round the corner.

On the 18th and 19th of April it began, and there was not a single moment when one heard no thud of enemy bombs and shells. We saw the first contingent of retreating men – our Russians. Worn-out, weary, torn, desperate men. They shouted 'Quickly, quickly the enemy's at our heels'. Then the orders came: leave everything, leave all equipment, leave all wounded and go eastwards without delay. Take what you can carry with you. Leave the wounded, leave them all.

It was in the evening of Sunday the 20th April. We seized our knapsacks and we began to go. And the wounded called out to us: 'Sestritsa, where are you going? Take me with you. Sestritsa!' from all sides it came. And we went quickly, we couldn't tell them we were leaving them. They took our skirts and pulled them, and shouted: 'You can't leave us!' Our doctors shouted: 'Go, go, go forward.' And we went. The wounded couldn't keep up with us, and we just left them there by the side of the road. And then their shouts turned to curses, and they cursed us for our cruelty in leaving them, we the sisters of mercy, leaving them to the enemy.

But we did, and by and by the retreat slowed up, fighting began again.

I couldn't understand how these soldiers stood up to all the dreadful snows of winter and the winds and the storms; their patience and endurance were unsurpassed. I have watched them go by dragging their tired, torn, dirty legs and feet along, scarcely able to support the big heavy knapsacks on their backs.

This was real war, of course, something new to this well-intentioned English girl, for real war blows men's arms and legs off, and splits open their bodies, and it's horrible. One of Miss Farmborough's soldiers had his jaw shot off. He couldn't talk, so they communicated in writing. It wasn't easy.

FLORENCE FARMBOROUGH I said, 'Your ikon. It's with the shirt that's been taken off you.' Yes, his head nodded. And I said: 'Listen, I will go and look for your ikon. Be quiet be patient. The ikon was taken away with your shirt this morning.' His eyes assented. So when I was free I went with one of my orderlies into a little hut and there were a heap of dirty, blood-bespattered shirts. I looked through nearly every one of them and the orderly helped me, but I couldn't find it. I would have given all I possessed to have found it for him.

I didn't go back to him that evening. I don't think I dared. I wanted him still to have hope. But the next day I went and they were being sent to the Base. And he looked at me, I could see his eyes questioning, and I had to shake my head. He made no sign. When the janitors come to lift him up from the stretcher he didn't even make a gesture. I knew he was resigned.

Sometimes we would sleep out in the open, but sleep was not always permitted because of the bed-louse and the flea. Our head orderly Smirnov told us: 'Sestritsi, if you want to get rid of all that disagreeable livestock, smoke makhorka.' 'But what is makhorka?' 'Makhorka is the soldier's tobacco. It never fails.'

Our tent boy rolled it up for us in little bits of paper and we were each given a cigarette of makhorka. We puffed it all round our blanket and under the pillow, but somehow the makhorka didn't act, we had headaches and we felt miserable.

All this time Miss Farmborough was working, as it were, as a sort of ex-officio war photographer. Wherever she went she carried a great wooden 1914 style glass-plate camera, with her tripod and the lot – which of course she could never have done had she not been accepted in the field as part of the officer-class, the people who had access to communications back to the capital. Taking the actual pictures must have been the easiest part.

FLORENCE FARMBOROUGH Sometimes in the midst of developing, a knock would come at my door: 'In five minutes we are leaving.' Good. I leave everything as they are. Turn out the developer. Pack the plates undeveloped, push them away somewhere. Those that were developed couldn't be taken, they were wet. One night I had marvellous luck; I had developed a dozen of them, and they were all beautiful and very successful. I lined them up along the pole at the bottom. But at night came a strong wind, and my plates fell face downward on to the sandy floor.

The Tsar's Army was now flagging desperately. The Plan was wrong; the equipment was wrong; the whole thing was no good. The soldiers didn't have the arms to fight with.

FLORENCE FARMBOROUGH There were many different kinds of munitions sent to them. Among them were bullets of Japanese make which would not fit their rifles. Then rifles were sent and they too were of a wrong make, and they were useless. I've personally seen men bring with them great cudgels out from the forest. When their rifles were useless, and the bayonet was useless without the rifle, they would go for the enemy with these cudgels. One soldier told me that he relied more on the forest than on the equipment sent by the military staff.

When we got to the Russian frontier all of us agreed, surely now the enemy would stop, he dare not pass into Russia. I remember Annushka, our little sister, weeping quietly. I said, 'Annushka, it will be all right, they won't come in to Russia'. She said, 'Florence, they will come when they are ready. They will murder our men. They will demolish our homes, they will devastate our land. I know they will come.'

So I left her. A few minutes later many wounded arrived. When I saw her she was a different person. She had her own private emotions completely under control.

Now the armies had with them that phenomenon of the 20th century: the refugees – the human debris. These refugees, Polish and Russian, were driven like sheep before the conquerors. Their sufferings were far, far worse. One refugee told her a nightmare story . . .

FLORENCE FARMBOROUGH I said to this man: 'Tell me, I know it's dreadful, but tell me.' He said: 'There's that man, a very good man, he loved God, and he was married. And on the road, a little boy came, a baby boy, he'd always wanted a son did Ivan Ivanovich. He was so glad, so happy. But she died.' So I said, 'And what happened?' He said, 'He buried them.' I said, 'Buried *them*?' 'Yes, I helped him dig the grave. We put her in, and he took the living child and put it on her breast. And I said to him "Ivan Ivanovich, what are you doing?" and he on to me like a wild savage beast, "Dost thou think I can suckle him? Dost thou think that he can live?

What is he to me without her?" And when he told me that he went on, 'And you know, Sestritsa, he loves God.'

This was only one terrible story among thousands of individual disasters. In 1916 the hapless Russians were sent into the attack once more. Miss Farmborough's unit was posted to the South-Western Front, far away in Romania. The nurses were not to know, obviously, the great gulf that was appearing between the Government and the people, the disintegration of authority, the impending collapse of the centre. The nurses were unaware of any of these huge developments far away; they were now desperately busy looking after the wounded pouring into the makeshift field hospitals.

One awful dilemma that faces any military nurse is that men with really bad stomach wounds must not be given water, although those are the patients who cry out for water all the time. Florence Farmborough had such a patient, thirsting desperately – and her experience had to fight with her compassion.

FLORENCE FARMBOROUGH I thought: if I give him water he will die, but he will die contented. If I don't give him water, he will die, but he will die tormented. I gave him the mug, he tipped it up and over his face and into his mouth, and I heard it being swallowed in big gurgling sounds. And then I knew what I had done. Almost immediately a terrible thing happened. From his mouth came a whole stream of dreadfully discoloured liquid. It came from his swollen, torn stomach and intestines and it flowed all over the sides of the stretcher on which he was lying. I went to the door and said 'Come quickly, come quickly, I think he's dying.' Ivan Ivanovich our *feldscher* said: 'Have you given him anything to drink?' I said 'Yes, I gave him something to drink. I had to. He was tormented with thirst.' And Ivan Ivanovich said, 'Well, you've killed him'.

After the orderlies had taken him away I went quickly to my tent, I felt I must be alone. When I went there Mamasha was there, the last person I wanted to see. She was so undemonstrative, I did tell her because I had to tell someone, and I said 'Mamasha, I've been accused of killing a soldier, he was dying and Ivan Ivanovich told me that I had killed him'. 'Tell me about it' she said, and I explained what had happened. Mamasha looked at me and said quietly, 'Florence, don't take it so deeply to heart. Had I been you, I would have done exactly what you did.' I just fell into her arms sobbing, but she put her arms round me and comforted me and I felt much better after that.

Even now a handful of crack regiments remained – the Cossacks, the élite of the Tsar's Imperial Army, the Guards of Russia.

Far away in Petrograd and Moscow the Russian social order that these Cossacks represented was dissolving, but still Miss Farmborough and the other nurses were remote from the revolution, still part of the officer class, with the privilege of access to the centre.

FLORENCE FARMBOROUGH Practically every week there would be liaison officers travelling to and from Moscow to our unit, and they would take any letters, my photo plates, anything we'd care to send to our friends. They brought my letters from home. One day I had sixteen letters from home.

Now, of course, different news was coming back from the capital in Petrograd and the great city of Moscow. This was 1917; this was the year of the Revolution, this was the end of the House of the Romanovs. There to Florence Farmborough among the soldiers it seemed very far away from the German war.

FLORENCE FARMBOROUGH Rumours were rife always, but they only bewildered us. We had seen nothing definite, not a thing in the Press, and no-one could answer our questions. And then things were made plain because from the military headquarters I received a remarkable document. It's probably the only one existing in the world today. It is the manifest of Tsar Nicolas II, proclaiming that he had found it difficult to continue at the head of the Empire, and that he was wishing to pass all the responsibility over to his brother, the Grand Duke Michael. He writes 'As it is difficult for me to part from my beloved son who is in delicate health, I have decided that he shall be freed from all inheritance'.

At dinner I remember that evening, some dozen or more, and we were silent. No-one could say anything. We didn't know what to say. For me it was dreadful, I felt more of an alien at that moment than at any time. He was not my Tsar, but he was their Tsar, and I was in their country.

But the Tsar was gone, and his Court and his dominion; the Empire of all the Russias was overthrown and never to return. The news was now of a Provisional People's Government, and its Minister of War was one Alexander Kerensky – the first of the populist leaders, the half-way man, so soon himself to be overthrown and exiled but in that spring of 1917 the undoubted man of the moment. One day Kerensky came to Sister Farmborough's sector of the front to address the soldiers.

FLORENCE FARMBOROUGH Kerensky mounted the steps and stood on the platform in full view of all the assembly. I was bewildered, I couldn't believe it was Kerensky. He was very young looking. He had a small oval face, shortish hair brushed tightly back, a dark blue uniform, but no emblems, no insignia, no decorations. He was just a plain, everyday man. Kerensky did not speak for very long, but not for a moment did he stop or stutter. The words came with a clear flowing movement, and everyone listened, spellbound. The soldiers' faces were rapt with wonderful expressions. The older ones, the younger ones, the middle-aged ones, all the same.

They recognised in him not only a great patriot, but a great and able leader. They shouted: 'We will follow you. We will go with joy and gladness into the trenches and fight for our Mother Country'. And then he descended the steps and in a moment the crowd had enclosed him.

But there were others against Kerensky, many others, with a harder line and a more uncompromising cause, the heralds of Lenin and his Soviet of Soldiers. They too toured the front with the simple message to the soliders: stop the war. Florence Farmborough heard one of them with a sense of shock.

FLORENCE FARMBOROUGH He was telling them that they were free men, their lives were their own, and they must not forfeit them by fighting any more. The war must come to an end. The soldiers listened. Many of the older ones quite aghast, the young ones with growing interest, growing enthusiasm. He too was a great orator, he too knew that these simple, guileless people could be led this way and that by the sheer power of oratory, and he went straight ahead. He told them, 'You have a free country. Liberty is yours. If you wish to throw away your life it's up to you, but as you are young and strong I would suggest that you go home, throw down your rifles and enjoy your freedom with your homefolk.' And that is what they did.

One day we were besieged by some young soldiers. They demanded bread, white bread. They demanded all kinds of things. Mamasha came quickly on the scene. They began to be very aggressive, and Mamasha stood her ground. There must have been fifteen or twenty of them, standing round looking sheepish, and trying to look very valiant. Mamasha was the brave one. She accused them of being traitors to their country. She said 'Who are you? A lot of illiterate boys – village boys.' She said, 'You can't even hold a gun. If you think you're going home, what will your mothers say to you? Won't they accuse you of desertion?' She spoke so vehemently, almost like those mothers themselves.

But on the fighting front there was nothing left to do; the war was evaporating; there were no longer any armies of the Tsar. The nurses got their orders to make their way back to Moscow. It must indeed have been a daunting journey for a handful of young women crossing South Russia, fearful even of their own soldiers.

FLORENCE FARMBOROUGH They were drunk with drink, and liberty. The horses had been stolen, so on we marched with this wall of soldiers. I was on one side of Mamasha, Annoushka on the other. The others came behind. Doctor Rachel, or Rakhil as we called her, a wonderful woman doctor from Odessa, with a sister on either hand. We passed on with great difficulty, pushed and jostled, but there was no alternative, we had to go with these deserting soldiers. Mamasha begged us to be silent, because if they heard a woman's voice they began to insinuate all kinds of evil things. Some of those would glare at us and demand where we were going and what right we had to be with them.

As we went on my long skirt – we had very long skirts in those days – caught on my boot. For one second only, I relinquished Mamasha's arm and stooped down to pull away my skirt. When I looked up I was alone. Even now I remember that dreadful moment. All round me soldiers pushing, jostling. I had to go with them this way, that way. I called out, 'Mamasha'. No answer. Then I called out, 'Anna, Annoushka!' And then I heard a most wonderful voice. It said: 'Florence!' and through the crowd, forcing her way through that human wall came Doctor Rakhil, Doctor Rachel, the new woman doctor from Odessa. She seized me and I seized her. An overpowering sense of gratitude came over me because I knew we were together, and I was terribly afraid of being alone.

Florence Farmborough, now separated from her friends, somehow got to Odessa, and somehow found her way to Moscow, where her story had all begun. And now she knew she had had enough, she knew now that she had to go home to England.

Before her stretched a journey across what is almost half the world – 27 days in a grinding train across Siberia to the Pacific, to Vladivostok.

FLORENCE FARMBOROUGH They said, 'There are no trains'. I said, 'But the trains are running on the Trans-Siberian Railway?' 'Only goods trains.' 'Well,' I said, 'I'll go by a goods train'. They hummed and hawed and I told them, 'Listen. If you're not giving me a ticket to go by train, I shall go back on foot.' Of course it was ridiculous stupidity to say a thing like that, but I really did want them to know that I'd made up my mind to go home. Finally they told me there was one more train, a goods train, composed of trucks, similar to our cattle trucks, and that was running via Smolensk and Omsk and going straight to Vladivostok. I said, 'Then I will take a ticket for the last Siberian train'.

The days passed, still on our journey. I was quite content. I wouldn't have minded if it had lasted several months, because I came under the healing influence of Siberia. I would sometimes stand on the little platform at the back. Miles and miles of white land, covered with snow. Its soothing quietness was like a tonic to me. Within a few days I was feeling as though I had never seen suffering.

As we neared Vladivostok we were wondering: What will happen to us? We shall be under the Bolshevik regime. What will happen? Will there be a British Consulate? As we came nearer the town, we saw the Bay of Vladivostok. In it there were four men-of-war. One of them we spied flying the Union Jack. I simply can't tell you our feelings at that moment. We were almost overwhelmed with gratitude. We knew we had come home.

Two Kinds of Life

Queen Charlotte's Birthday Ball, 1939.
Lady Wharncliffe and her daughters, Lady Diane and Lady Barbara Stuart Wortley.

ONE: WHEN ONE CAME OUT

In the summer months in the years before the last war, the daughters of the very best families in the land were driven to Buckingham Palace to be Presented at Court – to be formally introduced to the King and Queen.

This was the climax of a very special summer. These girls were Debutantes, making their debut into smart society. It was called 'Coming Out'. After 1939 there were no more Presentations at Court in the evening.

Among the two hundred or so girls Coming Out in 1939 were: Katharine Ormsby Gore, presented by her mother, Lady Harlech;

Dinah Brand, presented by her aunt, Lady Astor; and Christian Grant, presented by her mother, the Dowager Lady Grant of Monymusk.

CHRISTIAN GRANT I didn't have very many clothes, probably one, two, three, four, five evening dresses.

KATHARINE ORMSBY GORE You had what was known as a cotton frock which you'd wear probably until about tea-time, unless you were going to the races, and then you had a silk frock which you wore, you know, till dinner time. Cocktail parties had only just come in, so you wore this silk frock, and in the evening you came back and changed.

DINAH BRAND It was mainly the evening dresses that were rather smashing. I had, I suppose, about eight of those for dances and the rest was quite simple, not at all sort of grand, except for the ball gowns.

But clothes were only part of Coming Out. Before each debutante, stretched a first summer in society. At 17 or 18 they were now no longer schoolgirls but eligible young women. For six months they were to be carefully steered through the London Season, that unchanging calendar of social events that runs from spring to late summer. Ascot and Henley, the 4th of June at Eton, and almost every night a private dance. There you might see and be seen for the first time as part of society, but only if your mother permitted. Almost every girl who came out had a dance given for her. Details were published in *The Times* and *The Tatler*. Of course, there were rules to be observed. Before your dance your mother's friends each threw a dinner party for some of the guests. There friends and fellow debutantes might safely meet a select number of suitable young men.

CHRISTIAN GRANT We'd all turn up at the hostess's house about 8 o'clock in the evening, all us girls feeling rather shy and excited and all the young men in their white ties and tails, and we'd stand around rather nervously eyeing each other and drinking glasses of sherry because one wasn't given anything like gin or whisky in those days.

Then we'd all be ushered into dinner and the food was usually absolutely delicious. During dinner one would make very determined conversation with the person on the right and on the left because the man on one's right and left were honour-bound to dance with one at the dance, so one was sure of at least two dances. Then one would look up and down the table and see if there was anyone else one rather fancied. After dinner we'd all go off in a group to wherever the dance was being held, and sometimes some of the young men had their own cars. It was very dashing if one was taken to the dance by a young man in his own car.

KATHARINE ORMSBY GORE When you arrived at the dance, as you

came up the stairs they gave you a programme with a little pencil attached to it. This was with all the numbers of the dances. Then the young gentleman of the day rushes up and said, 'Would you dance with me number seven, or number three?'

DINAH BRAND If you were keen on somebody you hopefully filled it up from 5 to 10 with the same person, or if you were trying to avoid somebody you'd say sorry, I can't do that one, no can't do that, can't do that.

KATHARINE ORMSBY GORE I used to write it rather illegibly, and if someone asked one later I'd sometimes write the other name over the top and then when they arrived you used to say, 'How awful of me, I'm terribly sorry. I thought it said Henry and it does say William.'

CHRISTIAN GRANT Sometimes if one wanted very much to be asked to dance by some young man and he hadn't asked, one would write a few completely fictitious names in against the numbers, so one could then pretend that one's card was full. When he came along and said 'Have you a dance free?', you said, 'Well, I haven't really, but perhaps I don't have to dance with this one.' You'd cross out the fictitious name and write in the name of the man you'd really been longing to dance with all the time.

KATHARINE ORMSBY GORE There were people who were very kind and would ask you always and then occasional ones. I'd divide them into flirts, certs and wayside pleasures, and wayside pleasures were people who you didn't know very well and were a sort of added joy to one.

CHRISTIAN GRANT And then the exciting moment would be when one heard the band start in the room we were actually going to dance in and it always had the most electrifying effect. And then one looked anxiously around hoping that the young man who'd asked one for the next dance would turn up and claim one. There was this dreadful thing of being stood up.

DIANAH BRAND If there was a gap and you weren't dancing with anyone you pretended that you had to go down to the loo with the girls, that you were very busy talking to them. Actually you were filling in time.

CHRISTIAN GRANT The supper dance was always something one had saved for one's very favourite young man because one didn't only dance with him, one sat and talked with him.

And when the dance was over, our mothers would scoop us up and take us home, but if the mother went home before the end of the dance the dinner hostess was supposed to be honour-bound to take one home.

DINAH BRAND My nanny used to come, woken up by the alarm clock and set out in the early hours of the morning to come and collect me or my father's chauffeur, Mr Crisp, used to wait outside in the car till I was ready to come home. And we used to sort of rattle home in the dawn.

CHRISTIAN GRANT If one was feeling frightfully wicked, and one thought one could get away with it, one made an arrangement with some young man that five minutes after one was dropped back home he would arrive in a taxi or his little car and take one off to a night club and the dinner hostess, of course, never knew. It was supposed to be the height of wickedness to do this.

KATHARINE ORMSBY GORE I remember once climbing out through a conservatory and down the stairs with a great friend of mine and two young men and we went to a night club. It was rather a disappointment to me. I don't know quite what I did think I was going to find there – rather a disappointment. It was rather dark and looked rather grubby to me.

CHRISTIAN GRANT Some of the night clubs had cabarets, but even then, the people in the cabarets were completely clothed. It wasn't very daring, but I confess to being frightfully shocked by it. I was watching a group of girls dancing and I suddenly realised that the top half of their dresses were slightly transparent, and I was horrified at the wickedness.

It was a great thrill to have one's hand held by a young man. If a young man held my hand in a taxi I used to write it in my diary.

DINAH BRAND I wasn't aware that people were scheming for one to be swept up and married to a lord or a viscount. However, I suppose it must have been in the picture, because that was why we were all coming out really, to meet the right young men.

CHRISTIAN GRANT There was a type of young man, and after his name on the list was written N.S.I.T. and that meant 'Not Safe In Taxis' and under no circumstances would a mother allow her daughter to go home with a man with these terrible initials after his name.

DINAH BRAND Heaven knows what they were going to get up to, but the worst, I suppose. Then there was the sort of rather sweaty, podgy boy – I suppose he was only about 18 – and he was known as M.T.F. – Must Touch Flesh. There was a long sort of whispering 'Watch out for him – M.T.F.'

KATHARINE ORMSBY GORE And there was Ascot. We went to stay with Lady Astor at Cliveden, and that was great fun because there were about 20 of us, all quite young.

DINAH BRAND In the morning we'd probably play tennis or go out walking and then we'd get dressed up into our smartest clothes and the boys in top hats. In the hall laid out on silver trays were gardenias for the girls and carnations for the boys to wear in their lapels or on their dresses. And then we used to go off after lunch in a fleet of cars.

CHRISTIAN GRANT The country dances were the best, because they were given by people who had houses big enough to give that sort of party. So they usually had big gardens, and the gardens used to be floodlit and the fountains turned on. One used to wander about in these rose gardens with the nightingales singing and the moon and the distant sound of music.

DINAH BRAND But again, very much chaperoned. You didn't go off in, or at least you were supposed not to go off in, fast cars with young men without anybody there. Of course, if you had the chance you did.

KATHARINE ORMSBY GORE From about half past three to four in the morning you could have breakfast, bacon and eggs and sausages and kedgeree. You seemed to eat an awful lot. Then you had strawberries and cream or whatever it was. It was rather indigestible, looking back – kedgeree and strawberries and cream.

CHRISTIAN GRANT There was always this terrible problem knowing what to tip the servants because some of these houses had quite a large indoor staff. We would have liked to have given them some sort of present but it was sometimes quite difficult to find it out of our pocket money.

Then the Presentation. One's presentation dress was at that time the most wonderful dress one ever had, really only ranked second in one's mind to one's wedding dress. With my pink brocade dress I had a matching pink brocade train, just like a bride would wear, long white gloves with little pearl buttons at the wrist and a lovely sort of drooping spray of pink carnations to match my dress. No bag of course, so if one's nose shone, it just had to shine. And the three Prince of Wales feathers which were sometimes very difficult to fix. One had to hold them on with a mass of Kirby grips and hairpins and little bits of elastic. No jewellery of course, absolutely nothing, not even a pair of earrings because it was considered very bad form for girls to wear jewellery. Their mothers could wear everything they'd got.

The lights always had to be kept switched on inside the car because – it sounds awfully conceited – the people wanted to look at us. There were always a lot of people outside the Palace, on the days of the presentation. So we all sat in these little lit up boxes all the way down the Mall, waiting for the gates to open, and one didn't look to right or left, one looked down at one's little bouquet and hoped for the time until the gates were opened. When the time came, the gates of the Palace were opened and this long crocodile of cars drove in carrying the mothers and the daughters.

KATHARINE ORMSBY GORE I remember being very surprised that Buckingham Palace was really two houses. I hadn't realised that there was a courtyard between. There was a red carpet in the middle and soldiers standing all the way up the stairs.

DINAH BRAND We were sitting in an ante room on gold chairs and the wait was very long. It was three hours, I think.

KATHARINE ORMSBY GORE Then you went through a door into the throne room, and the King and Queen were sitting on a dais on two chairs with the Gentlemen of Arms behind them. They called out your mother's name and said 'To be presented' and then your name and then your mother went forward until she got opposite the King and Queen and then she curtsied and then you curtsied. And I remember thinking, 'Well, I won't put my head down' which you were told to do, 'because', I thought, 'I'll never get so near to seeing them again, so I'm going to have a jolly good look while I'm here.'

DINAH BRAND One very comforting thing for me was that on the platform with the King and Queen was my uncle, who was then Admiral of the Fleet at Devonport and he was a little man with a very amusing face, and as I did my curtsey I looked up and saw him wink at me. That was the best moment of the whole day.

I shall always remember what a really fantastic sight it was. The room was marvellous, the jewellery, the dresses, the platform or the dais where the King and Queen and all the entourage were, unforgettable.

KATHARINE ORMSBY GORE Everybody of course knew the war was coming. People have a great illusion that we didn't know. We very much did know it was going to happen. During that summer I remember going to Red Cross classes and First Aid classes.

CHRISTIAN GRANT Six months after I was presented I was working on the shop floor of an aircraft factory. I was a thing called a bench fitter and was banging about with a hammer and a hacksaw and that kind of thing – ten hours a day.

TWO: WHEN ONE WENT IN

Things were otherwise for Gergana Taneva.

Gergana was not living in Mayfair, but in Central Europe. She was one of the tens of thousands who for one reason or another, or none, got swept up by the Nazis and locked away during Hitler's war. She was also one of those who, by luck and fortitude, managed to survive.

Gergana Taneva was the teenage daughter of political refugees from Bulgaria. She had already had many restless years with her parents – first in Yugoslavia, then in Italy, then further north in France. She came to learn a new language in each country. During the war she had to speak German. (After the war she was to marry an Englishman and learn one more language.) But when in 1939 the Germans began the bombing of Warsaw, Gergana was a young girl living in Poland.

GERGANA TANEVA I was just sixteen – was I? I was just sixteen when my mother was killed in the bombardment and there I was, all alone, without any relatives, without any connections. My father was dead for a year. For a while I was living with an old lady who took pity to a girl all alone in an absolutely destroyed city.

In the ruins of Warsaw then it was the Jews who walked in real fear. Gergana was not a Jew, but one day she stepped into a nightmare that was to last exactly five years. Early in May 1940 she was out walking with some friends.

GERGANA TANEVA Then suddenly there was German voices and we found that the street from all sides were closed, a big lorry first drove in front of us, and then another one, another one . . . about five or six of them. We started to run. But every possible escape route cut off.

Gergana and her friends were thrown into the lorries. They were taken overnight from Poland to Germany and put to work as young slave labourers in Munich.

GERGANA TANEVA In the factory where I worked I got to know some Dutch students, they were picked up in Amsterdam just as I was picked up in Warsaw. We got involved in a student organisation. They were printing leaflets and were helping to distribute them.

That was taking a terrible chance. It could have led straight to the concentration camp. She landed in Munich jail on suspicion, but was released. The next time she was picked up she had anti-Nazi leaflets on her.

GERGANA TANEVA I was brought again to the same prison and the same floor, but a different small cell. After a few days' interrogations they brought me a paper to sign, that I'm going to be sent to Auschwitz. Well, the name Auschwitz in 1940, wasn't yet as horrible as it was later so. But I thought, 'Oh no, I'm not going to Auschwitz. It's quite out of the question. I can sign anything they like, but I'm not going there. I shall think of something.'

The girl I was with in this cell said, 'Don't be silly, this is quite impossible, how do you want to escape from a German Headquarters of the Police? Don't be naive: this is impossible.' I said, 'I will think of something.'

I had long dark curls on my shoulders and innocent eyes and looked quite – perhaps quite respectable. So I didn't have any proper plan, but I thought it might be possible to escape when they are feeding us in the later afternoon. That moment the telephone in the office next to my cell rang and the wardress went in. So I thought: this is my moment. I jumped out of the cell and opposite on a windowsill – I saw a big piece of paper which I grabbed. Looking at it carefully I walked down the corridor, slowly, pretending to look like an office girl, a typist or somebody. This was all unprepared – just happened. Now I had to go downstairs – I thought, when I meet somebody downstairs who knows me – because I was second time there – so I'll be for it. On the stairs I met an enormous policeman who greeted me very politely and went past, so that was all right. The tricky part was the ground floor, which was the men's department, and there were policemen in front of every cell door. But I knew the glass door which led to the entrance hall. So I went very very slowly. It seemed to me like ages. I walked step by step, very slowly looking at this list, I can remember the list very vividly. It was a list of gypsies coming from Salzburg being brought to Auschwitz to be destroyed.

At this door a plain clothes Gestapo man was standing. So I just marched through that door and said 'Auf Wiedersehen, Heil Hilter!' And he said, 'Auf Wiedersehen, Fräulein!' And there I was in the Headquarters where you can go, you know, and fetch passports and I don't know what.

Then the enormous policeman again came towards me, and I said, 'Excuse me, please, where is the exit here?' And he said, 'Just left, down there.' I said, 'Thank you very much!' – and run down the stairs, and there I was outside. They tell me that was the first and last time somebody escaped from the Munich prison.

Her 17-year-old innocence had pulled off the impossible: she was out of Munich jail. But now, if the Gestapo found her, she would certainly go to Auschwitz.

Some anti-Nazi Bulgarian students gave her contact addresses in Sofia. She was smuggled out of Germany with a party of Balkan factory workers who were making the long trip home for Easter. She disguised herself in men's overalls. Her fellow-travellers were helpful – especially one elderly Bulgarian shepherd.

GERGANA TANEVA I was sitting in a corner next to the window, and I woke up and saw at the end of the corridor the torch which the railway men carried, so I shook my Bulgarian shepherd and said: 'Look, they're coming.' It was just in time. I couldn't do anything but pull my legs up and huddle in the corner and Minco the shepherd, who wore a shepherd's cloak, enormous, just stood there like this with his cloak spread over me. I was very small and thin, so it didn't make any difference really. So this was the first part of my journey.

At the time Bulgaria was an ally of Nazi Germany. It was going to be very dangerous indeed for Gergana without identity papers. But at the next frontier her luck held again. A train full of Bulgarian soldiers stopped alongside them.

GERGANA The soldiers were very bored, I suppose. Our train was full of bearded, dark, bearded, dirty men, not being able to wash for days: and suddenly in one of the windows there was a young girl with long curls falling over her shoulders. So they started to joke and call to me, 'Oh girl, why don't you come with us? Do come with us! It's much nicer here . . . !'

I got sudden inspiration. So I said to my shepherd: 'Thank you very much Minco I'm going to do that, I think.' And he said, 'Yes, that's the best thing to do.' And since there wasn't any platform he let me down and lifted me up to the military train, and at that moment it started to move. So I walked into the compartment when I saw the young soldiers there, and I said, 'Well, here I am: You wanted me to come!' Well, they weren't very happy I must say: they were rather put out, and said, 'We didn't mean it, it's not allowed, you know, that you're here!' So I said, 'It's too late now, the train is moving.'

By the time we arrived at Sofia, I was discovered by an officer on the train. He ordered me out on to the platform. He handed me over to an officer in a Bulgarian uniform and a steel helmet, who said, 'Come with me.'

Now here I am in Bulgaria, and caught. My heart sank, and I followed him, and after a while I was wondering – where is he leading me? Because he wasn't leading me towards the guards room. He was leading me to the left luggage department. I thought: 'My goodness, it's somewhere behind there they're going to hand me over to the Police.' But no, he went past it and was leading me to the lavatory and I thought: 'Oh my god, what's going to happen now.' Right into the lavatory. I was really frightened. But on the other side of the lavatory there was a glass door to the street. He brought me out and he said, 'Do you know Sofia at all?' I said, 'No'. He said, 'Well, good luck to you,' saluted smartly and went back.

I knew that I wouldn't last very long without any papers. One of the students in Munich gave me three addresses which I had to learn by heart, and I was told to go to a certain newspaper stand and ask for them. And so I went there and I said, 'Excuse me,' – my Bulgarian wasn't very good – 'Do you know a man called that and that?' And he shook his head. I said, 'Do you know this one?' He shook his head. 'Well, do you know this one?' It was the third and last, and he shook his head. I said, 'Oh my god, what now?' Turned round and started to walk off and he screams after, 'Miss, what do you think you're doing? Why you going away?' And then I realised, of course, in Bulgaria, shaking head is 'yes', and nodding is 'no'.

He knew them of course, but they weren't any use. One was arrested: one was interned. And the other was in the ghetto, he was Jewish, so it wasn't much help.

Bulgaria was my birth country, but I could hardly speak the language. I was arrested by the Bulgarian police for having no identity papers. I began telling all sorts of stories.

I knew only one thing, that I must not tell that I'd escaped from Germany, because they had an alliance with Nazi Germany. And since I wouldn't tell them anything which made any sense they were rather puzzled. And that's where the funny part really stops and unpleasant starts, because when they didn't get anything out of me – they had to find ways not very pleasant. And when they led me to another interrogation through the building, there were young people standing with their faces to the wall everywhere, and ghastly screams from every room, and I was rather frightened. And then suddenly I see two big, tall men with green uniforms and they shout: 'That's her!' It was my bad luck that my Gestapo men from Munich was transferred to the military police in the South of Bulgaria on the Greek frontier.

They took me after two days back to Germany. I was put in solitary confinement and given a full treatment – what the Gestapo say it.

They sent me to the women's concentration camp at Ravensbruck. Only about three women in four died there. My first job was the mortuary.

Every day the S.S. lorry would come and would swing the bodies on to the lorry and they were carted away to the crematorium where they were burnt. First three days were rather disturbing because I couldn't get used to it. I'd seen some bodies during Warsaw bombardment but still, it was rather a frightful job. After a few days everybody got a number and a triangle – the political prisoners had a red triangle: Jehovah's Witnesses – violet; Russenschund – what do you call the Russenschund? – somebody who was committing a sin against the purity of the German race. That meant somebody who was married to a Jewish person. They were green, which were regarded as professional criminals. And black, the asocial persons – they were like prostitutes, gypsies, people who didn't like to work and so on. So we had all a triangle on our left sleeve and a number. I've got a number still: 207 14.

This box did belong to a girl who was going to the gas chamber and I just had time to write her number: her number was 69,624 and she just threw it at me as they were disappearing out of the gate and I'm keeping it. And this is my number . . .

Number 207 14 was now eighteen years old, and a political prisoner with a red triangle. She was to be in Ravensbruck for more than three years.

GERGANA TANEVA Two oldish German ladies who already had eight years of hard labour behind them, they told me, when I didn't feel like washing in cold weather: if you don't wash you're not going to survive. You must, because this is the first step to apathy. You have to fight. And so we washed every day. It was really very, very hard on us, but we did. People who didn't wash started to steal, started to despair, got diseases, died, were taken away to be destroyed.

Groups with strong beliefs – say, Jehovah's Witnesses, or Social Democrats or Communists or militant Catholics, or for that matter Nationalist groups like the Poles who kept together for patriotic interests – they had the most chances to survive because they had something to make them keep going. There were young students, schoolgirls who just interrupted their schooling when the war broke out in Poland. We had the best teaching capacities from whole Europe in the camp – women professors from Sorbonne, and best scientists from Holland and Norway and Hungary – whatever. So young girls had opportunity to use every free moment, you know, to scribble something on a tiny little paper, you know, and learned algebra and trigonometry and biology and history and languages. Languages were easy because you had so many different nationalities. I personally learned Russian in Ravensbruck.

We had about thirty children there – quite small. Some were born there, but some were about five, six, seven, eight years old, so, of course, we all did things for them.

Then I got a job in Siemens Factory. The famous firm of Siemens specially built a factory nearby the camp. They were earning quite a nice profit from the slave labour. So prisoners were driven every day through this tiny town of Furstenberg.

Everybody knew about it. Everybody saw women without hair; women with striped clothes; women dragging bodies of their dead comrades who died during the work, or bitten to death by S.S. dogs – what do you call them – Alsatians. They were specially trained to deal with women. They were trained to grab at the breast and at the crutch. The people from this little town saw it all. And everybody knew these concentration camps.

As the war went on the camps became more and more crowded. The S.S. looked continually for new ways to thin the numbers out. At the women's concentration camp of Ravensbruck they made what were called 'selections'.

GERGANA TANEVA Selection was an event of which everybody was deadly afraid. It was really a matter of death and life. Old women were blackening their hair with soot. We were getting beetroots from the kitchen and rubbing into our cheeks. I just had typhus shortly before the last selection, so I was very pale and my legs were like sticks, and I hardly could walk, so I thought when I just drop in front of them, then it's finished for me.

So I made myself beautiful red cheeks with a piece of beetroot. Everybody said: take a piece of string and tie the wooden shoes to your feet. Because they had to see if we can run, not only walk; if you can run it's all right. The ones who were allowed to stay alive went out one side and the others were going to the gas chamber and were put on the other side. So you can imagine when the mother was standing on one side, and her daughter on the other. But don't imagine that there was lots of screaming and wailing. We learnt not to be vocal about things. But it's a nightmare, when you think about it. So I managed to run with my thin legs and my few tufts of hair which I had after the typhus and there I was. But many lorries were driven on that day away into the gas chamber.

People tend to have the impression that the S.S. who were murdering and beating and torturing people were some kind of sadists. They had wives and kiddies at home, and Christmas we could hear them singing sentimental songs of Christmas. And afterwards they would come and kill some people and beat some women. They were quite ordinary people: if you put them in civilian clothes on the street you wouldn't see anything different about them.

We knew, of course, that the war was going to be lost by the Germans, it was clear to everybody. But we really could not believe that we're ever going to die any different than hunger, in the latrine, or beaten to death, or in a gas chamber. We just couldn't imagine that, because they spent years to convince us that we are not really people, that we are just a great big heap of unworthy human manure, you know, not worth keeping alive.

1945 – January, February, it was clear that something was moving; guards started to be friendlier, and there were rumours that we were going to be driven out of the camp.

The rumour soon became reality. Late in April, with the Allied Armies advancing into Germany on all fronts, the gates of the camp were opened, and huge processions of starving women prisoners flanked by S.S. men were marched off towards the North.

GERGANA TANEVA For miles and miles, you could see only women. Not all in striped uniforms because towards the end they didn't have any more stripes. But a big wide cross was painted with white oil paint. So you couldn't escape with that, even if you wore civilian clothes. So we were marched through woods and through villages.

The news spread – we didn't know whether it was true or not – that they're going to drive us to the sea, put us on an old ship, and sink us, as they did with many men prisoners from Sachsenhausen. So we decided to walk as slowly as possible, because we could already hear the shooting of the artillery from the East: it was the Red Army.

And suddenly somebody nudges me and says: 'Look,' and we discovered there's no S.S. around us, we were all quite alone on this dark road – no soldiers, no S.S., nobody around us and we got frightened.

This sudden freedom was almost too much for the 21-year-old Gergana. She was with about five hundred women and a few children. They were afraid that there might still be German troops somewhere about and they huddled together for a while in an old cemetery. Then Gergana was sent off with another German-speaking girl to find a safer place for them all to hide.

GERGANA TANEVA We met a young German in a Luftwaffe uniform on a bicycle. I asked him, 'Do you know is there any forest up here . . . in the neighbourhood?' And he said, 'I am looking myself for one.' And suddenly there was a big S.S. man behind us, and a group of Sachsenhausen concentration camp men being driven past. He bellowed at me, 'Where are you coming from?' And immediately when I heard that voice, I was standing there like a jellyfish. I said, 'We've been driven from Ravensbruck and left on the road.' And in that moment, the young soldier picked up his bicycle and hit this man on the head. I don't know what happened then because we started to run into the cemetery.

And so we spent all night bringing these women to this small wood, and really when it started to get light we were all well covered. But towards afternoon the children got frightfully thirsty, they didn't have anything to drink for days. They started to cry, they couldn't stand it any more. So we got a blanket each from the children to cover our stripes – so we're not conspicuous. We went down the hill and there was a little hut with a pump in front of it. We made sure there were no Germans around and we took some water from this pump.

And it must have been about ten or eleven – frightful shooting started – artillery. From East and from West. We really in the middle in the fire line. Tree tops were falling on us. Many people were hit from our group and some men were killed. Then it was still again, and we didn't wait, we just got up and galloped down the hill, like wild horses down. An enormous German emerged from the bushes: 'You crazy females, where are you running? The Russians are there!' So we said, 'Thank you, that's just what we want.'

And right past him and there was the road and the Russian tanks. And there was a tremendous kissing and embracing. There was one young soldier who didn't have anything to give us, but he wanted very much to do something for us, so he took a bottle of eau de cologne and sprinkled on us, just to be nice to us. I found myself with enormous piece of fat sausage in my hand, and just couldn't swallow anything. 'A moment,' he says, ran to his tank and filled up very thick glass three-quarters with a liquid and said, 'Drink!' I said, 'No, I daren't.' He ran again to his tank and got some water from his radiator and filled this glass with water and said, 'Now you can drink'. So I said, 'What, vodka mixed with water, what's going to happened to me?' So I gulped it down. I don't remember anything after that. So when I woke up it was a brilliant May morning. It was May Day 1945.

Acknowledgement is due to the following for permission to reproduce illustrations; Exeter City Library, p26; Len Potter, p30; Radio Times Hulton Picture Library, p50, p84; Ian Keil, p89; *Flight*, p95; Alex Revell, p106; *The Glasgow Herald,* p120; *The Tatler*, p140

These are the 'Yesterday's Witness' programmes from which these scripts have been edited.

Directed by Stephen Peet:
The Levant Mine Disaster
Two Victorian Girls
The Great Blizzard of 1891
The Tithe War
To Paris – by Air
Five Years' Nightmare
Zeppelins over England
The Burston School Strike

Directed by Michael Rabiger:
Prisoners of Conscience
Breaking the Silence
A Remnant of a Feudal Society
The Battle of Cable Street
A Cause Worth Fighting For

Directed by Ian Keill:
The Narrow Boat Men
The First War in the Air

Directed by Patsy Meehan:
The Great Scuttle
The Jarrow Crusade

Directed by Charles Mapleston:
The Abandoned Island

Directed by Jane Oliver:
The Burning of the Bombing School

Directed by Anna Benson Gyles:
The Last People of St Kilda

Directed by Christopher Cook:
English Nurse with the Tsar's Army
Coming Out in '39

Series Producer: Stephen Peet